WINNING LOCAL
AND
STATE ELECTIONS

WINNING LOCAL AND STATE ELECTIONS

The Guide To Organizing Your Campaign

Ann Beaudry
Bob Schaeffer

THE FREE PRESS
A Division of Macmillan, Inc.
NEW YORK

Collier Macmillan Publishers
LONDON

The Free Press
A Division of Macmillan, Inc.
866 Third Avenue, New York, N.Y. 10022

Collier Macmillan Canada, Inc.

Printed in the United States of America

printing number

1 2 3 4 5 6 7 8 9 10

Library of Congress Cataloging-in-Publication Data

Beaudry, Ann E.
 Winning local and state elections.

 Bibliography: p.
 Includes index.
 1. Campaign management—Handbooks, manuals, etc.
2. Electioneering—Handbooks, manuals, etc.
I. Schaeffer, Bob. II. Title.
JF2112.C3B416 1986   324.7'8'0202   85-28066
ISBN 0-68-486377-4

To
E.G.B.
—A.E.B.

and

E. & D.J.
—R.A.S.

CONTENTS

In-Kind Contributions
Conclusion

9. **Volunteers** 187

The Volunteer Coordinator
The Plan for Volunteer Activities
Organizing to Handle Volunteers
   Preparation of Volunteer Materials
   Recordkeeping
      PLEDGE CARDS
      VOLUNTEER DAILY SCHEDULE SHEET
      VOLUNTEER REQUEST FORM
   Setting Up the Headquarters
Recruiting Volunteers
   Recruiting Volunteers for Leadership Roles
   Recruiting Friends and Associates
   Recruiting Message
   Ongoing Recruitment
   Follow-Up
Managing the Volunteer Program
   Making Assignments
   Volunteer Training
Monitoring the Results
Sustaining a Volunteer Organization

ACKNOWLEDGMENTS

While writing a book seemed to be the most solitary task I've ever undertaken, I gratefully acknowledge the support of a community of friends and family who made it possible.

The first of those friends is Jean Weinberg. She shared a vision of involving progressive and pro-choice activists in grass-roots campaigns and encouraged me to begin this project. Also, my heartfelt thanks to the network of friends across the country from the Conference on Alternative State and Local Policies. They are many of this book's success stories.

I wish to especially thank Bob Schaeffer, who collaborated with me over the three years this book was in the making. He has truly been a partner from conceptualization to final edit.

Though it may be unrecognizable without the battle metaphors, Bill Zimmerman's invaluable contributions are reflected in the chapters on campaign strategy and political media, and Paul Bennett's wit and wisdom contributed greatly to the fundraising chapter.

A special word of thanks to Barbara Guss, Christy Macy, and Teresa Horrigan, who helped proof the various drafts, and to Susan Moeller, whose design work helped greatly to structure the book. In addition, Herb Gunther, Tim Feder, and the staff at Public Media Center in San Francisco provided invaluable assistance through this book's many incarnations.

And finally, it would never have been published without the encouragement of Barry Bluestone.

None of the chapters has been previously published in the form they appear here. Portions of earlier drafts of material in this book were prepared as a training manual for the National Abortion Rights Action League, and I am grateful to them for their support.

Erwin Glickes and Grant Ujifusa of The Free Press were an indispensable help. They believed in this book and provided the suggestions, criticisms, and unflappable patience needed to make it become a reality.

Most of all I thank my family. They don't always understand what I do, but it is their love and support that make it possible.

The people who have contributed in the past fifteen years to my experience and philosophy of running campaigns are too numerous to mention here. But I thank these mentors. Their ideas fill these pages. The final responsibility for errors and excesses is, of course, mine.

Ann Beaudry
Boston

INTRODUCTION

This book is for candidates and their campaign staffs who want to win local and state elections. It was written for those high-volunteer, low-budget campaigns that are the very heart of our democratic system.

Contrary to Watergate and what many pros chronicle as a growing cynicism about politics, we see a growing grass-roots movement toward increased involvement in electoral politics. Community organizations that previously demonstrated on the steps of city hall are now fielding their own candidates for city council. Women who played key support roles in previous campaigns are filing their own petitions for elections. As challengers for school boards or county commissions, from town hall to the state house, citizen candidates of all political persuasions are becoming involved in races for elected office.

Every two years, more than 450,000 offices are up for election across the United States. More than one and a half million candidates seek these positions, many of them for the first time.

This book is designed to make that first step an easier one. In it we try to demystify the techniques of running a professional, well-planned campaign. Each chapter emphasizes techniques that are applicable for local races from school board to state senate and for those candidates whose list of friends is bigger than their bank account.

Our formula for winning is simple: *repetitive, persuasive communication with likely voters is the key to victory.* Each of the techniques described in this book is part of a coherent strategy to communicate your campaign message to a carefully targeted audience. In addition to step-by-step descriptions of campaign activities, we've also included many of the forms, checklists, sample letters, and press releases you'll need for your campaign.

We've provided the basic outline. Now it's your turn to adapt this guide to fit your local situation. With careful planning and disciplined implementation you, too, can *run to win.*

Ann Beaudry
Bob Schaeffer

WINNING LOCAL
AND
STATE ELECTIONS

DEVELOPING YOUR CAMPAIGN STRATEGY

Theme

Audience
Voting Behavior
Voter Opinions
Geography
Demographics

Delivery

Resources
The Candidate
People
Money
Time

Simply put, a campaign is a communications process. Whether you are running in a large state senate district or seeking a position on a small local commission, your goal is the same: to convey your message to voters in such a way that a winning margin votes for your candidate on Election Day. Any experienced campaigner will tell you this involves hard work, but the basic strategy for winning is straightforward: *repetitive, persuasive communication with your likely supporters.*

Your overall campaign strategy molds all of the separate components of your organization together to reinforce your message. In this manual we will explain how to set up and run the inner workings of scheduling the candidate, building a field organization, media, and fundraising. Because we've demystified these activities, you will find that many of the skills you already have can be successfully put to use.

However, good skills alone are not enough. To be successful, a campaign must have a well-defined communication strategy. Unfortunately, too many campaigns are designed by technicians rather than political strategists. Understanding the basic elements of voter communication strategy will help you develop a winning campaign. These are:

- Theme: What is the single, most important message to be communicated to the electorate?

- Audience: Who are the voters who can be persuaded to vote for you?

- Delivery: Which methods of communication will most effectively convey your message to potential supporters?

- Timing: When is the best time to deliver your message to targeted audiences?

- Resources: What resources are available to facilitate communication with your target audience?

We want to help you think through all of these elements in the context of your own campaign. Keep in mind that all of them are closely interrelated. Accordingly, assessments made about one will often affect the decisions made about all the others. That is why designing a winning campaign strategy is more an art than a science.

Let's look at each of the basic elements of campaign communication in more depth.

Theme

The most important element is the *theme*—the basic message the campaign will communicate to voters. Its purpose is to differentiate, to set your candidate apart from all opponents in the race. It is your answer to the voter's question, "Why should I support you?" The theme should capture the rationale for the campaign in a simple, dramatic, and persuasive way.

Anyone who decides to run for public office is likely to have strong stands on a number of public issues. But from the beginning, it's important to keep in mind that a campaign is not an exercise in persuading the voters to accept *all* your positions. Developing a winning strategy and designing an educational program for voters are markedly different undertakings. It is often necessary to sacrifice complexity in order to develop the campaign's primary message.

It's a mistake to confuse the laundry list of the candidate's positions on various issues with the fundamental theme that should define a campaign. While candidates should be prepared to respond to questions on a wide range of issues, they must have a single clear message that will convince voters. Then, all the components of the campaign can be designed to advance that message.

To understand why this is so, you need to know something about the modern communication process. We are all constantly bombarded by "messages" from newspapers, TV and radio, billboards, friends, and neighbors. This means that your campaign message will be competing not only against that of your opponent, but also against those from candidates in other races, commercials for detergents and soft drinks, and news reports of thousands of local, national, and international events. To screen out as much of this "noise" as possible, people erect protective barriers. Everybody blocks out hundreds of potential messages each day.

The chances of your message getting through is measured by what engineers refer to as the "signal-to-noise ratio." Research has shown that a simple, dramatic message is most likely to stand out from background noise and be received by an individual. Especially in the final weeks of a campaign in which many offices are contested, competition among signals aimed at potential voters is tremendous. Thus, the message that convinces voters to vote for your candidate must be extremely clear. Your "signal" must be short and easy to understand.

Two main factors should determine your campaign theme: policy issues that concern voters, and the personal characteristics and reputation of the candidate. Let's consider issues first.

Is there a big local problem, one that can be appropriately addressed by the office you are seeking? If so, that issue—a utility rate increase or a proposed school bond issue—can be developed into the major theme for your campaign. An incumbent may want to stress proven leadership in addressing such concerns, but a problem left unsolved by an incumbent is a good issue for a challenger to highlight.

A major national issue can also be used successfully in a campaign theme if research demonstrates a local connection. For example, the absence of plans for dealing with toxic wastes can be made a central local campaign issue if the candidate uncovers a little-known disposal site in the district. The key is to make sure the issue is important to local voters. One could say, for example: "Vote for Smith as though your life depended on it. She WILL clean up the Hoovertown dump."

It may also be possible to develop an issue latent in the voters' minds and intensify its importance. Such a strategy had a marked effect in the Santa Monica, California, city council elections in

1980. When research showed that more than 60 percent of the residents in that community were renters, campaign strategists for a slate of challengers made rent control their central theme. Their campaign communication dramatized the plight of longtime residents, especially the elderly, who were forced to move out because of escalating rents. Volunteers in an extensive door-to-door canvass distributed simple flyers with photos of senior citizens who had been evicted. By Election Day, rent control had become the dominant issue in the municipality and the pro–rent control slate won a majority on the city council.

The campaigners in Santa Monica learned from experience the distinction between a clear campaign theme and detailed policy positions. Two years earlier, activists in the same community tried to educate voters and garner support for their candidates by circulating fact-filled position papers on rent control. Their overwhelming defeat in the 1978 election was a marked contrast to their success in 1980 when the same issue was translated into a simple, graphic campaign message.

A campaign theme may also be developed around the candidate's personal or political characteristics. To begin, assess the major ways your candidate can be contrasted with the opponent in terms of style, experience, capabilities, values, and alliances with interest groups.

Can you run as an "insider" and capitalize on your experience? If not, can you portray your candidate as a fresh new face? Will you identify your campaign with that of other candidates for other offices, either as a "slate" or by joint endorsements? What emphasis will you give to your candidate's or your opponent's support by trade unions, the downtown business community, or community organizations? As you ask questions like these, consider not only what the perceptions are at the outset, but also how they can be developed during the campaign.

The initial assessment involves evaluating your candidate's strong points. It also requires analysis of the points on which your opponent may be vulnerable. Voting record research is a good place to start if you are challenging an incumbent or someone who has previously held elected office. Don't overlook such matters as a poor attendance record or a general pattern of unresponsiveness to constituents' problems. These may be more important in voters' perceptions than any particular issue position. In 1984, for example, twenty-eight-year-old John Houston, a first-time candidate, defeated a sixteen-year incumbent, the majority leader of the Massachusetts State Senate, by waging an aggressive door-to-door campaign that reminded voters they had not seen their senator in years.

Finally, your candidate might have special attributes or an unusual background sufficiently distinguishing to help shape the communication theme. It's not textbook civics, but the visibility of many first-time campaigns is increased because the candidate is a former astronaut, a well-known sports figure, or the spouse of a movie star.

To develop your campaign theme, you will have to find your own balance between issues and personal characteristics. Though we have tried to resist the temptation to use examples from national campaigns, a well-known presidential campaign best illustrates the point. In this case it's a negative example—the wrong mix of issues and perceived personal attributes. In the early stages of the 1980 campaign the Kennedy for President staff prepared a large tabloid for use in Iowa and New Hampshire. In bold letters the front page read: "THERE IS ONE ISSUE IN THE RACE FOR PRESIDENT." The two-page center spread was devoted to a full-page photo of Ted Kennedy and the words in giant type, ". . . LEADERSHIP." Three short paragraphs covered the senator's positions on a variety of issues, but the clear message of the piece—and the theme that was stressed from his November announcement through February—was a personal trait, leadership.

Obviously, campaign strategists thought the Kennedy image would contrast favorably with Carter's lackluster persona. However, by their choice of a theme, the campaign encouraged voters to compare the personal characteristics of the two candidates, which only heightened Kennedy's identification with Chappaquidick.

Contrast Kennedy's showing in the early primary and caucus states to his more successful performance after the famous Georgetown speech in which he emphatically delineated his policy differences with the President. With this first real substantive address, the campaign changed thematic horses in midstream. It could not, of course, stop the public and press attention given to Kennedy's personal history, but it did begin to create a positive counter focus around issues.

In developing your campaign theme, try to anticipate potential negatives and turn these into positives. For example, an extremely young candidate can stress new, innovative solutions while a senior citizen can emphasize experience and make age a positive attribute.

Jim Hightower's 1980 statewide race for Commissioner of Agriculture in Texas used humor to turn a potential negative into a positive campaign theme. In an opening campaign salvo, his opponent called Hightower an "agitator," referring to his ties to many activist organizations. To the delight of the press, Hightower's reply set the tone for his challenge to a three-term incumbent. "I welcome being called an agitator," he said. "That's what my grandmother used to call the thing in the center of the washing machine that went around and got the dirt out—and that's exactly what we intend to do in this campaign!"

Again, keep in mind that all the components of communication—theme, audience, delivery, timing, and resources—are interrelated. Be sure to take into account the campaign's resources and its planned method of delivery as you decide on your theme. Your message and your means of delivering it must reinforce one another. A high-powered, paid media campaign projects a very different image from a grass-roots volunteer effort no matter what the content of its message.

The proposed theme should also be evaluated in the context of the audience to which it will be addressed—the voters in your district. Remember, you can't sell wrinkle cream to teenagers, not even very good wrinkle cream. Therefore, always consider the demographics of your district. For example, a candidate who supports a school tax levy can win an election in a district that has a large percentage of senior citizens, but few campaign strategists would advise that as a major theme.

Audience

To win on Election Day, your communication must *convince your audience and motivate them to vote for you.* That's the ball game. The more precisely you define your audience and target your message to it, the more likely you are to have a winning campaign. Your strategy must consider the following four variables about your potential audience:

• Voting behavior

- Voter opinions

- Geography

- Demographics

Taken together, these variables will give you the best composite picture of your campaign's audience. Take the time to carefully research each one during the early stages of mapping out your campaign. You may find that in the process of developing this picture you'll come up with new information and perspectives that contradict the quick assumptions you may have made earlier—or that people may have told you—about your district.

Voting Behavior

The single most important factor in defining the audience for your campaign message is the past voting behavior of residents of your district. Analyzing turnout and voting patterns will help you narrow the potential electorate by identifying areas with population concentrations most likely to vote for you.

It may sound like heresy to suggest that you only need to communicate with those who are already favorable or who can be persuaded to be. In fact, this advice often doesn't sit well with many first-time candidates who feel they must knock on every door at least once. But in even the smallest campaign, the secret to success is repetitive, persuasive communication with your likely supporters, not casual contact with the entire universe of adults in your district. By narrowing the audience for your campaign communications, you can concentrate your limited resources where they will do the most good, which is produce the most votes.

Defining the most likely audience for your campaign is called "targeting." The simple methods of computation for targeting are described in detail in Chapter 2. Even those with math anxiety can perform them quite easily. Targeting should be completed in the earliest stages of planning your campaign.

Voter Opinions

A successful campaign theme emphasizes the candidate's priority issues that most closely match the key concerns of the targeted electorate. To find an optimum match, you must evaluate the opinions of the electorate in your district. There are many formal and informal ways to do this. Candidate coffees and voter canvasses provide good opportunities for two-way communication. The candidate can also consult with community leaders to identify key concerns of neighborhood residents as well as with representatives of important constituencies, interest groups, and organizations.

Depending on the size of your district, the amount of lead time available, and your budget, you may choose to conduct a poll to get a better understanding of voters' opinions. To do this, seek the help of someone experienced in designing surveys and choosing samples, possibly a political science professor from a local college. Volunteer interviewers can do a good, inexpensive job if the poll is brief. Remember to keep it simple. You are only interested in testing major campaign themes, not in compiling a detailed list of voter opinions on a wide range of public issues.

Geography

Where people live in your district is also an important factor. Among other things, geography limits possible campaign styles and, thus, has a major effect on the delivery of your message. Just ask anyone who's tried to conduct a campaign in New York City how difficult it is to conduct a door-to-door canvass in high-rise apartment buildings—the security system or doorman usually won't let nonresident volunteers in. On the other hand, the distance between houses in sparsely populated areas makes it equally difficult to personally reach voters. Some districts, however, may include a geographic mix. So to reach prospective voters directly, you may have to use a variety of tactics: door-to-door canvass in small towns or suburban areas, but mail or telephone contact downtown and in rural communities.

Geography is also important because it defines the main travel and assembly routes in the district. Traffic patterns can help you identify places where there are large numbers of people. For example, in a district with a high percentage of public transportation commuters, you can reach many voters with relatively few volunteers by leafleting bus, subway, or railway stations.

Issues of concern to residents may vary significantly among the neighborhoods or communities within your district. The targeting methods outlined in Chapter 2 will help you break your district down into smaller geographic units. This will allow you to fine tune your message by amplifying certain stands according to local attitudes.

Demographics

Another way to analyze your audience is demographically. Demography looks at voters not in geographic subdivisions, but as members of special groups with common concerns. Surveys such as the U.S. census give a profile of voters in a tract that includes information about age, race, education, income, ethnicity, home ownership, and employment patterns. Why are these important? Because group interests play an important role in determining the themes of the campaign. Obviously, the issues that concern blue-collar renters in an area with high unemployment will differ from those in a professional suburb where most residents are upper-income homeowners. Likewise, an audience with a high concentration of young families with children is very unlike one with a majority population of senior citizens or students.

Decisions about campaign style and methods are also affected by demography. In communities with many established formal groups your strategy may emphasize the endorsements from labor unions, community organizations, environmentalists, and women's or minority groups that will contribute volunteers and/or financial support. In some areas, you will need bilingual materials and volunteers for door-to-door campaigning. If your district has a high percentage of students, you will have to design campaign techniques appropriate to reach them. In general, understanding the demography of your district will enable you to tailor your campaign programs so that they will most effectively reach your targeted voters.

Delivery

Your campaign will deliver its message to voters in two basic ways: through direct personal communication (either by the candidate, surrogates, or volunteers) and nondirect, or mediated, communication (radio, TV, newspapers, brochures, billboards, and the like, including both free news coverage and paid advertising).

Your overall campaign strategy must outline how each of these delivery methods will be used. A host of techniques for direct voter contact are detailed in Chapter 4 on candidate activity and Chapter 5 on field organization. The campaign's capacity to obtain free press coverage and the extent of the paid advertising program are important to your campaign strategy and will be covered in detail in Chapters 6 and 7. The delivery methods your strategy chooses to stress will depend on the theme itself, the audience you are trying to reach, and the resources available to the campaign.

The important thing to remember is that all the methods chosen for delivering your campaign message should reinforce one another. Each should reflect the simple themes that you have chosen to provide repetitive, persuasive communication with your supporters.

To reach the voters you must also know what they read, what they listen to, and what they watch. What is the relative importance of the local 5,000-watt radio station or the local TV channel or the one affiliated with a major network? Here, a good understanding of the demographics of your district is essential. In St. Petersburg, Florida, with a high percentage of senior citizens, it may be more important to place ads or to have stories about the candidate in the local senior citizens' publication than in the daily newspaper. Similarly, a candidate for local office in Gary, Indiana, might discover that the local steelworkers' union publication reaches a greater percentage of targeted voters than the metropolitan daily.

Decisions about how to deliver your message must also take into account the resources you have available. If the campaign organization has enough money, you may decide to do direct mail that is personalized by interest groups. If funds are short but you have enough volunteers, you may decide instead to distribute literature door-to-door in targeted areas.

Resources

The final elements to consider in developing a strategy are the campaign's resources: the candidate, people, money, and time. Every activity included in the campaign plan involves some combination of these. And as anyone who has run a campaign can tell you, *resources are always limited and needs are always unlimited.* Only careful planning will help you allocate resources most effectively.

Many resources can be used interchangeably. The precise mix depends on how much of each resource you have and how you decide to allocate them. It's possible to run a phone bank, for example, using rented space and paid callers—it will cost about forty cents per call. Yet an all-volunteer operation out of private homes or donated space can do the same job for approximately one cent per call. A volunteer phone bank needs much less of one resource, money, but far more of another, volunteer hours.

Let's take a look at each resource.

The Candidate

A successful campaign is a team effort, but the central figure in developing the campaign strategy is always the candidate. As noted earlier, the candidate's priority issues, personality, and experience frame the major themes of the campaign. Contrasting the relative strengths and weaknesses of the candidate with those of the opponent will further shape a strategy that highlights the candidate most effectively.

Another key factor is the candidate's name recognition and reputation. A campaign for an "unknown" will have to utilize different techniques in the early stages than one in which the candidate is already well known to the voters. Your message cannot persuade voters until they know who your candidate is. Name recognition is always the first hurdle.

What about the personal abilities of the candidate? It's necessary to take stock at the outset. You can certainly build a winning campaign around someone who is less than charismatic—to be honest, few candidates are—but your strategy must emphasize your candidate's strong points. Good organizational planning must compensate for areas of weakness.

- Is the candidate a good public speaker who is persuasive with large audiences, or does he or she communicate more effectively in small informal gatherings?
- How successful will the candidate be in getting resources for the campaign—raising funds or recruiting volunteers?

The answers to these and similar questions will help to determine the most effective scheduling of the candidate's time and the style of campaign.

Another factor is the amount of time the candidate will make available for campaigning. A full-time candidate can obviously adopt a more flexible schedule than someone with a full-time job or someone with extensive family or civic obligations. The attitudes of members of the candidate's family must also be considered. Will they object to hours spent on the campaign trail, or do they plan to play an active role in the campaign? If your effort can count on a number of family members to do door-to-door canvassing or to represent the candidate as surrogate speakers, be sure to factor this additional resource into your communication strategy.

People

There are two things to consider as you evaluate the people resources in your campaign: the endorsements of key individuals and volunteers. Decide whose support will be important and begin lining up those endorsements early. These may be leaders of organizations that you will rely on for dollars and volunteers, or they may be well-known figures with such standing in the community that their endorsement is tantamount to the "Good Housekeeping Seal of Approval." Political leaders and other elected officials can also gain votes for you, particularly within their own constituencies. In many elections the early race to get endorsements helps to clear the field of potential candidates, with only those who have sufficient pledges of support officially announcing their candidacy. You are the best judge of who the key people are for your particular race. Remember, endorsements can help in several ways: not only are many voters guided by endorsements, but influential people can help raise money and recruit volunteers.

In most state and local races, motivated volunteers fill most, if not all, campaign staff roles. The smaller the race the more likely this is to be true. Volunteers are essential in a campaign whose strategy involves a high degree of direct contact with voters. Except in the very smallest districts, it's simply not possible for the candidate to meet each prospective voter in person.

Your estimate of the number of volunteers you will be able to recruit will significantly affect the planning of major campaign activities. To do this, begin with the network of the candidate's friends and contacts; then consider the members of organizations who will play major roles in the campaign. To this base, add an estimate of the number of voters who can be recruited through candidate coffees and other events.

As you do this, you should measure not only the number of people you can recruit, but also the talent or skills they bring to the campaign. People with specialized skills will be necessary in a few roles. For example, the success of the campaign fundraising plan will depend either on your ability to recruit finance committee members who have contacts with potential large donors, or on a greater number of volunteers who are able to run small-scale events or direct mail drives. A lawyer will also be needed to advise the campaign on election laws.

Prior campaign experience may be helpful, but it is often not the best measure of a volunteer's effectiveness. The financial director of a citizens' organization or someone with business experience has valuable skills that can be easily transferred to the job of campaign treasurer. The greatest assets that volunteers bring to a campaign are their enthusiasm and their commitment.

As with all the other resources, the value of volunteers in a campaign can be multiplied many times by good organizational planning that ensures they are well used.

Money

The techniques outlined in this manual are specifically designed for high-volunteer, low-budget campaigns. Many campaigns have been successful even though they were outspent two, even three, to one, but it is a myth that candidates or organizations can run even highly motivated volunteer campaigns without money.

California State Treasurer Jesse Unruh is usually credited with the saying, ''Money is the mother's milk of politics.'' That's understandable wisdom in a state where Tom Hayden's successful 1982 campaign for the state legislature set a new record with campaign expenditures totaling $1 million. Those figures may seem astronomical compared to the costs in your state, and indeed, there is a wide variation across the country in the average expenditures for state and local elections.

One of your first research efforts should be to find out what similar local campaigns have spent in preceding elections. Then realistically estimate the amount of money that will be available to you. This is not the wish-list amount, but a reasonable figure that you can use in your campaign planning. Compare this figure to what has been spent in previous races and to what you expect your opponents will raise.

Time

Time is the only resource you cannot alter. With a large number of volunteers, you can design activities to raise more money. Conversely, if you have a lot of money you can hire staff or compensate for a small volunteer corps by reaching voters through direct mail or a paid media program. But neither people nor money can buy more time. A campaign that gets a late start faces especially severe limitations. In such a case there may not be sufficient lead time to prepare direct mail or organize fundraising events, so all fundraising may have to be done by personal solicitation.

In a campaign, time is usually measured by counting the number of days until the election. However, other factors may limit the amount of time available for campaign activities. For example, no matter how early it starts, a campaign in a district with a mid-September primary has only the first two weeks in September to reach returning college students. Consider, too, such factors as midsummer vacations and school or religious holidays that may make reaching voters more difficult. Will the number of volunteers who are available for your campaign decrease or increase during certain time periods? Consider these factors as you allocate the time resource during the campaign.

Conclusion

Once you've reviewed the basic elements of campaign communication, you'll be ready to craft your own answers to these five basic questions:

- What is your theme or message?
- Who is your audience?

- How will you communicate your message?

- When?

- With what resources?

Your answers will define the overall strategy for your campaign. Think about the questions and your answers as you go through this handbook. Remember, no matter how large or small your campaign, careful design at the outset will pay off Election Day.

2

TARGETING YOUR AUDIENCE

Remember the golden rule for high-volunteer, low-budget campaigns: repetitive, persuasive communication with your likely supporters. Here we want to talk about the second half of the rule: identifying your likely supporters.

Our major premise is that the more carefully you define your audience the more effectively you can concentrate your efforts to reach them. The reason for audience definition is simple: the people most likely to vote in your election are those who regularly vote in similar elections. And their voting patterns will most likely resemble those of previous years. Never get the idea that your campaign is going to magically transform the electorate.

In any campaign with a clearly defined strategy not all areas should be treated equally. For example, you should expend fewer resources in low turnout areas and in your opponent's stronghold than in areas with a high percentage of potential supporters. Attempting to attract voters in an area where your prospects are minimal is a waste of valuable limited resources.

Mind you, that's not the correct approach if you can afford to saturate the electorate with paid advertising. But in all the races for the more than 450,000 state and local offices across the country, such expensive media campaigns are rare. So, unless you know at the outset that money will be no object in your campaign, it is essential to identify the areas in which voters who are most likely to vote for you, or who can be persuaded to vote for you, reside. Limited campaign resources can thus be focused where they are likely to produce maximum results.

Identifying priority areas is accomplished by a process called "targeting." You may have heard of any one of a number of sophisticated computer targeting programs that have been used by congressional or national campaigns. The most sophisticated of these, such as Claritas, which was perfected by Washington, D.C., political consultant Matt Reese, make extensive use of census tract data. Of course, if your resources permit, you can hire a political consulting firm to come in and do targeting for you. But you don't need to be a professional to adapt targeting methods to an appropriate level for your campaign. In fact, at the risk of being expelled from the profession for divulging trade secrets, we intend to demystify the targeting process so that it can be successfully used by even the smallest campaign. If you follow the steps outlined in this chapter, gathering election information and performing the necessary computations can be accomplished with only a pocket calculator in just a few hours.

Targeting does not predict the turnout or voting behavior in a specific precinct or area. It is a statistical measure of past voting patterns that has proven to be a reliable indicator of future voting behavior in the same area. By targeting you can identify those areas with the greatest concentrations of nonvoters and voters who consistently support candidates from the other political party. These areas should be a low priority, if they receive any resources at all. And likewise, targeting will pinpoint those areas where the greatest concentrations of potentially favorable and persuadable voters are located. *These are the voters who represent the margin of victory in a campaign.* It is in these high priority areas that you want to concentrate your campaign communications.

Good targeting is both an art and a science. Though analysis of election statistics is the cornerstone of targeting, the data generated must always be combined with demographic factors and sound political judgment to fine tune the results and apply them to your campaign—a fact that cannot be stressed too heavily. You may want to seek out someone with extensive knowledge of the district to help you interpret the numbers and target your priority areas.

The initial stage of targeting involves three basic tasks: obtaining election statistics, selecting comparison races, and performing calculations. Each step is described in detail for the two types of targeting done for a general election: intermediate targeting, and precinct targeting. These same two types are applied differently in primary elections. Let's talk about general elections first.

Obtaining Election Results

Obtain a copy of the complete election returns from the general elections held in your district for the last four years. Get the vote totals for all candidates for each office on the ballot broken down by the smallest subdivision reporting—usually a precinct. Also get the most recent voter registration totals, broken down by party if your state has partisan registration. Do not use statistics from races that go back more than two general elections. The average American moves once every four years, so voting habits in areas with a high degree of mobility will change over time.

The office of the secretary of state or the Board of Elections in the state capital is the primary source for most election returns and the voter registration figures you will need for a statewide or state legislative race. To obtain election results broken down by smaller subdivisions or precincts for targeting for local races, it may be necessary to contact the appropriate local offices, most often the county or town clerk or the County Board of Elections. Do not be discouraged if you are told that the material is not readily available in printed form. Election results are a matter of public record in every state and must be made available to you, though you may have to pay for photocopies or, in some cases, arrange to hand copy the figures from the official file.

A secondary source is the local newspaper. Check the library or archives at the newspaper for the editions issued immediately following Election Day in past years. These numbers though unofficial, are usually highly accurate.

Selecting Comparison Races

The first step is to select previous races that can be used to measure past voting behavior in your district. All your targeting computations will be based on the results of these races. The goal here is to choose races for comparison that are the most analogous to the contest you face. You can choose a single comparison race or two or three and average the results. The latter process is a bit more complex, but it is likely to give a more reliable picture of the voting patterns in your district. For that reason, we've used the averaging method in all of the examples that follow. Choose carefully. The judgments made in selecting comparison races will determine how accurate your final targeting or priority ranking of precincts will be.

Review all election returns from the previous four years. Then, choose comparison races that are most similar to your own. For example, if you are running for the state legislature, statistics from previous state legislative races are best. If you are challenging an incumbent, consider previous races that person has been in. Also, avoid comparing those races that were highly controversial. An emotionally charged ballot referendum or initiative may significantly skew the turnout results. Likewise, races that were dominated by a particularly strong candidate's personality are not good baselines either. These races are often atypical and will not reflect normal party preference or general voting patterns. For example, in the first Chicago mayoral race after Richard Daley, no candidate would have been well served to use previous mayoral election results for comparisons in their targeting. The same holds true following long-term office holders such as Erasmus Corning, mayor of Albany, New York, for more than thirty years, or Boston's mayor, Kevin White. Information from at-large city council races or perhaps county offices may be all that you can go on.

Also, be sure to note if there is a significant difference between the number of voters who turn out in your district in presidential and nonpresidential election years. If turnout differs greatly you can eliminate one variable by choosing comparison races from an off-year if you are running in an off-year or, conversely, from a presidential election year if you are running in a presidential election year.

Most targeting is usually done by breaking votes down along party lines, especially in a general election. You can also measure voting behavior along ideological lines if candidates can be clearly identified as progressive or conservative in the races that you choose for comparison. If initiative and referendum ballot issues play an important political role in your state, consider them in choosing comparison races. If the major theme of your campaign is very similar to a "yes" vote on a recent ballot measure, an analysis of the returns from that vote may provide valuable information. In this case, count the votes supporting the ballot measure in the same manner as you would count votes for a candidate similar to yourself in a comparison race.

Targeting Priority Areas

There are two kinds of targeting to determine priority areas: intermediate level, which is often called "percent-of-effort targeting," and precinct targeting. Percent-of-effort targeting provides a general overview of the major subdivisons in your district. These may be towns, counties, or wards, depending on the size of the district. We have used wards in our examples. For each comparison race, you will determine what percent of the candidate's vote was compiled in each major part of the district. The index measures the relative electoral importance of each subdivision in previous races in order to provide a guideline for planning what percent of your campaign's effort should be expended in each of these areas. This form of intermediate, or percent-of-effort, targeting is used to apportion general campaign activities such as the candidate's time schedule and local advertising purchases.

Precinct targeting provides a more precise analysis of the smallest subdivision in the district, usually a precinct. The process involves identifying precincts where concentrations of voters who exhibit certain characteristics reside. For example, you can identify those precincts with a high percentage of voters who normally support your party (or the opponent's party), or precincts that usually have a high turnout of voters on Election Day. Precinct targeting is highly specific and the priority ranking of targeting precincts is the basis for determining the allocation of resources in the campaign's direct voter contact programs, such as telephone and door-to-door canvassing or direct mail.

Use the worksheets in this manual to record the computations for each comparison race as you go through the step-by-step procedures that follow. You'll be surprised. It's easier than it looks at first glance.

Percent-of-Effort Targeting

Percent-of-effort targeting identifies the likely percentage of your total vote that will come from each subdivision so that you can allocate the appropriate percentage of your resources to each subdivision. For example, if an area contains 30 percent of the potential Democratic vote, a Democratic campaign should allocate approximately 30 percent of the candidate's time and other resources to that area. Likewise, an area with only 10 percent of the potential Democratic vote should receive about 10 percent of that campaign's efforts. Once you have completed percent-of-effort targeting you may even decide to "write off" some subdivisions and not expend any resources there because in the past it has not produced any significant support for campaigns similar to yours.

To begin, analyze the comparison races you have chosen and calculate what percentage of the total vote in the district was cast in each subdivision for the candidate who is most similar to yourself. The formula is:

$$\frac{\text{\# votes cast in single ward for candidate}}{\text{\# votes case in entire district for candidate}} = \text{ward's \% of vote}$$

The following examples illustrate how to apply this formula to three comparison races. To help you, we've included a worksheet on page 24 on which to record all your computations. Simply extend it if you have more than eight wards or subdivisions.

First: for each comparison race, perform the following computations for a single subdivision:

1. Determine the total number of votes cast in the entire district for the comparison candidate.

2. Determine the total number of votes cast in the ward or subdivision for the comparison candidate.

3. Divide the number of votes in each ward or subdivision for the comparison candidate by the total number of votes in the whole district for the comparison candidate. Record this percentage on the worksheet.

WORKSHEET FOR PERCENT OF EFFORT TARGETING

	Comparison Candidate #1	Comparison Candidate #2	Comparison Candidate #3	Average
Ward 1	Votes Ward 1 $\dfrac{\Box}{\text{District Total } \Box} = \Box$ %	Votes Ward 1 $\dfrac{\Box}{\text{District Total } \Box} = \Box$ %	Votes Ward 1 $\dfrac{\Box}{\text{District Total } \Box} = \Box$ %	$\dfrac{\Box + \Box + \Box}{3} = \Box$ %
Ward 2	Votes Ward 2 $\dfrac{\Box}{\text{District Total } \Box} = \Box$ %	Votes Ward 2 $\dfrac{\Box}{\text{District Total } \Box} = \Box$ %	Votes Ward 2 $\dfrac{\Box}{\text{District Total } \Box} = \Box$ %	$\dfrac{\Box + \Box + \Box}{3} = \Box$ %
Ward 3	Votes Ward 3 $\dfrac{\Box}{\text{District Total } \Box} = \Box$ %	Votes Ward 3 $\dfrac{\Box}{\text{District Total } \Box} = \Box$ %	Votes Ward 3 $\dfrac{\Box}{\text{District Total } \Box} = \Box$ %	$\dfrac{\Box + \Box + \Box}{3} = \Box$ %
Ward 4	Votes Ward 4 $\dfrac{\Box}{\text{District Total } \Box} = \Box$ %	Votes Ward 4 $\dfrac{\Box}{\text{District Total } \Box} = \Box$ %	Votes Ward 4 $\dfrac{\Box}{\text{District Total } \Box} = \Box$ %	$\dfrac{\Box + \Box + \Box}{3} = \Box$ %
Ward 5	Votes Ward 5 $\dfrac{\Box}{\text{District Total } \Box} = \Box$ %	Votes Ward 5 $\dfrac{\Box}{\text{District Total } \Box} = \Box$ %	Votes Ward 5 $\dfrac{\Box}{\text{District Total } \Box} = \Box$ %	$\dfrac{\Box + \Box + \Box}{3} = \Box$ %
Ward 6	Votes Ward 6 $\dfrac{\Box}{\text{District Total } \Box} = \Box$ %	Votes Ward 6 $\dfrac{\Box}{\text{District Total } \Box} = \Box$ %	Votes Ward 6 $\dfrac{\Box}{\text{District Total } \Box} = \Box$ %	$\dfrac{\Box + \Box + \Box}{3} = \Box$ %

Sample computations for the first ward for three comparison races are:

First comparison race:

$$\frac{450 \text{ votes cast in ward \# 1 for Candidate A}}{3,000 \text{ votes cast in district for Candidate A}} = 15\%$$

Second comparison race:

$$\frac{320 \text{ votes cast in ward \# 1 for Candidate B}}{3,200 \text{ votes cast in district for Candidate B}} = 10\%$$

Third comparison race:

$$\frac{360 \text{ votes case in ward \# 1 for Candidate C}}{3,000 \text{ votes cast in district for Candidate C}} = 12\%$$

Second: average the percentage figures from each comparison race to find the percent-of-effort index for the subdivision:

$$\frac{15\% + 10\% + 12\%}{3} = 12\% \text{ Percent-of-Effort Index for Ward \# 1}$$

(Note: If you only use two comparison races, remember to divide by 2 in computing the average.)

Third: repeat these computations for each ward or subdivision within the district.

Once you have completed all the computations, list the wards in descending order of their average percent-of-effort. You can use the chart on page 26. This chart will help you assign a priority ranking to each subdivision within the district. (Note: Because you are rounding off percentages and determining an average percentage for each subdivision, the total of the percentages for all subdivisions in the district may be a few points greater or less than 100 percent.)

Fine-Tuning the Results

Targeting begins and ends with political judgments, with many computations in between. The statistical measures derived from

WORKSHEET

WARD #	Results of Percent-of-Effort Targeting (Rank in descending order)
Ward _____	
Ward _____	
Ward _____	
Ward _____	
Ward _____	
Ward _____	
Ward _____	
Ward _____	
Ward _____	
Ward _____	

targeting should supplement and not substitute for political experience in evaluating the district. Your first judgment comes in selecting which previous races you will use as a comparison to your own. That, as previously discussed, involves many subjective decisions. Once the statistical phase of the targeting has been completed the campaign leadership must combine the results with knowledge of the politics and demographics of the area before final targeting decisions are made. Overriding considerations may surface that cause you to upgrade or downgrade some areas depending on their importance in the overall campaign strategy. Before you determine their final priority ranking and the percent of effort to be allocated to each ward, you should consider several factors. For example:

- Is there a large concentration of union members in an area, or an active community organization that has endorsed (or opposed) the candidate?

- Are there media outlets or press possibilities in one area that could affect voters in a larger area?

- If the residents in an area are strong supporters of a single issue, does this increase or decrease the likelihood that the candidate will find support there?

- Is your opponent's home ward popularity so strong that you should concede those votes in developing your campaign plan? Or coversely, is dissatisfaction so high that you might make unusual gains?

Remember, it's important to strike a balance between the mechanical technique and careful political judgment as you fine tune your targeting results.

Precinct Targeting

The purpose of this kind of targeting is to give you a precise profile of the voting behavior of each precinct so you can concentrate your direct contact with voters in those precincts where the potential is the greatest. That profile is derived from the measurement of four basic characteristics in each precinct:

- Size
- Turnout
- Performance
- Persuadability

Each characteristic provides important information that is useful in deciding which methods of voter contact will be the most effective in each precinct. First we'll describe the computations necessary to measure each characteristic, and then discuss their uses in targeting specific campaign programs.

A precinct targeting form appears below; use it to record the results of your computations for each precinct. To simplify matters, round off the numbers as you record them so they will be eas-

PRECINCT TARGETING FORM

Precinct #	Size	Turnout	Performance	Persuadability

ier to compare. If necessary, make additional copies of the form to cover the total number of precincts in your district.

Size

The most important single characteristic of a precinct is how big it is. For the purposes of targeting, the applicable measurement of size is the total number of registered voters in a precinct. This is the total of *all* registered voters, not just those that are registered in your party.

Total # of registered voters in precinct = Precinct size

Turnout

The second characteristic of a precinct is the percentage of registered voters who turn out to vote on Election Day. Based on the assumption that past trends will be repeated in the current election, turnout measures from previous elections are good indicators of the approximate numbers of registered voters within a precinct who are likely to cast a ballot in the upcoming election.

Voter turnout is the one characteristic that varies greatly between presidential and nonpresidential election years. There are higher turnout figures in presidential election years because many people vote only in that election. Thus, to ensure greater reliability of your turnout measurement, choose comparison races from years that are analogous to your own. For an even more reliable turnout measurement, you can average the turnout percentages from two comparison races for each precinct.

To calculate the turnout percentage, obtain the total voter registration figures for each precinct and the total number of votes cast in each precinct in the comparison race. (Note: This is the total number of votes cast for all candidates in the race, not just for the candidate from your party.) Divide the vote figure by the total registration figure.

$$\frac{\textbf{Total vote in the precinct}}{\textbf{Total registration in the precinct}} = \textbf{Precinct turnout}$$

Performance

Performance is the measurement of the partisan voting patterns in a precinct. It is used to determine the normal percentages of party strength in a precinct. In the example below the votes cast for the Republican candidate in a comparison race are used to measure the percentage of normal Republican vote in a precinct, which can be called the Republican performance quotient.

To determine the precinct performance percentage, select three comparison races that are analogous to your campaign. For each race identify the number of votes cast for the candidate of your party in each precinct. Divide that figure by the total number of votes cast for all candidates for the same office in the precinct.

$$\frac{\text{\# of votes cast in precinct for Republican candidate}}{\text{Total \# of votes cast in precinct for same race}} = \frac{\text{Precinct}}{\text{performance}}$$

Compute the average of the three performance percentages derived from the three comparison races to determine the overall performance of each precinct.

Persuadability

Persuadability measures the degree of independence in the voting patterns within a precinct. This measurement identifies concentrations of voters who do not vote a straight party ticket but tend to split their votes between parties in a single election, or to switch from party to party in successive elections. The trend toward split ticket voting and switch voting is increasing as voters are becoming increasingly independent and loyalty to the major political parties lessens. These split ticket voters are open to the persuasion effects of a particular campaign and represent important potential votes for your candidate.

Persuadability is measured by computing the difference between the percentage of votes cast in a precinct for a party's most popular candidate and the percentage of votes cast in that precinct for the same party's least popular candidate. To make such comparisons you may select two candidates running for different offices in the same election year, or two candidates in different election years. The former indicates what is called "split ticket voting''; the latter indicates ''switch voting.'' Each provides a good measure of persuadability.

For each precinct, identify the candidate from your party who received the highest percentage of votes and the candidate from your party who received the lowest percentage of votes. To calculate the percentages of their vote, divide the vote total for each candidate by the total number of votes cast in the precinct for all the candidates in that same race.

$$\frac{\text{\# of votes cast in precinct for candidate}}{\text{Total votes cast in precinct in that race}} = \frac{\text{Candidates \%}}{\text{of the vote}}$$

Next, subtract the low percentage (that cast for the least popular candidate) from the high percentage (that cast for the most popular candidate) to determine the persuadability measure for the precinct.

$$\frac{\text{\% of votes cast in precinct for most popular candidate}}{- \text{\% of votes cast in precinct for least popular candidate}}$$
$$\text{Precinct persuadability}$$

Repeat the same process for each precinct with two other races that indicate split ticket voting or switch voting. The average of the two percentages of precinct persuadability will yield a more reliable measure.

Ranking Precincts in Priority Order

Now that you've developed a profile of each precinct, you can use that information to rank them in priority order for the voter contact programs of the campaign. These programs—such as door-to-door canvassing, phone banks, literature distribution, and direct mail—are all designed to communicate persuasively with the voters. To rank precincts in priority order you need to consider the characteristics of size and turnout in addition to the precinct persuadability measure. The highest priority precincts for your voter persuasion efforts are those that are characterized simultaneously by large size, high turnout, and high persuadability. For example, given two precincts with equally high measures of persuadability, the larger precinct would have a higher priority ranking because it would have a greater number of persuadable voters. Similarly, if two districts have equal measures of persuadability, you would give a higher ranking to the precinct in which the turnout was greatest because more persuadable voters in that precinct are likely to vote.

Refer to the chart of precinct characteristics that you have completed on page 28. To approximate the number of persuadable voters in each precinct, multiply the three figures for persuadability, turnout, and size for each precinct:

Persuadability × turnout × size = # of persuadable voters

Once you have a figure for each precinct, list all the precincts in order from highest to lowest. The highest ranking precincts, those with the greatest number of persuadable voters, should be the top priority for your voter persuasion efforts.

If you have a large number of precincts, it often helps to divide them into three or four groups on the basis of their priority for voter persuasion activities. This will make the system more manageable. For example, the highest precincts should be grouped together, the second level of precincts within a certain range should be grouped together, and so on. These groups allow you to lump together the lowest priority precincts, which will not receive any attention from the voter persuasion program unless there are sufficient resources.

Targeting information also seems more manageable if you translate the numerical rankings onto a color-coded map. Use one color to shade precincts in the top priority group, other colors to shade precincts in each of the other groups. This map helps campaign leaders quickly see the priority given to each area.

Targeting Primary Elections

Targeting methods in primary elections differ from those for general elections. Only in the case where you can identify consistent factions within your political party (e.g., liberal versus convervative, reform versus regular) can you choose comparison races from previous primaries that will give you accurate measurements of performance and persuadability. For this reason, these two measures are very seldom applicable when targeting for a primary election. If you can clearly identify intraparty factions in primary elections, compute precinct performance and persuadability in the same manner as described earlier for the general election. When selecting comparison races from previous primary elections, use the vote totals for the liberal or the conservative candidates within the same party in the same manner as you would use Democratic or Republican figures in a general election.

In all other cases, the key measurement to use when targeting primaries are size and turnout. The applicable number to use to measure precinct size for primary targeting is *not* the total number of registered voters in a precinct, as is the case for general elections. Instead, the correct measurement is the number of people in the precinct who are eligible to vote in your party's primary. You can obtain this information from the Secretary of State or the municipal registrar of voters. Eligibility will depend on the election laws in your state. In a closed primary state, eligibility may be limited to the voters registered in that party. If voters registered as "Independent" are eligible to vote in either party's primary, you will have to add the number of independent voters to the number of voters registered in your party to obtain the total number of eligible primary voters in each precinct.

Voter turnout in primaries is generally lower than in general elections, so be sure to use comparison races from previous primary elections when you are computing turnout figures for each precinct. Measure the percentage of turnout by dividing the total number of primary votes cast in each precinct in a comparison race by the total party registration in each respective precinct.

To target your priority precincts for voter contact programs in a primary race, simply multiply size by the turnout percentage. This will give you an estimate of the number of voters in each precinct likely to vote in your party's primary. Rank the precincts from high to low according to this number. Those precincts with the largest estimated number of primary voters should be the highest priority for your campaign efforts in a primary election.

Dealing with Boundary Changes

Following the 1980 census many states reapportioned their congressional districts. In addition to these changes, which are made every ten years, many also changed the boundaries for state legislative districts. Local election authorities may also make periodic changes in precinct boundaries. If there have not been any boundary changes in your district within the last four years, you may happily skip this section. If the boundaries have changed, they may pose a special obstacle in conducting the targeting procedures, which assume you can trace the voting behavior of a given precinct through the last two elections. But when precinct lines are redrawn, the precinct figures have to be converted to ensure you are using measurements that will apply to the current campaign.

Converting precinct information to fit current boundaries may seem to present a difficult problem, but it's well worth the work to gain this valuable information. Oftentimes the changes involved are not substantial, which simplifies the conversion. You may need to seek the advice of someone with experience on the effects of reapportionment. One such person is a member of the state commission or an aide to the legislative committee involved in drawing the new districts. They will know about boundary changes applicable to your legislative district and their implications. Likewise, seek help from officials at the local election authority about changes in municipal precincts. They can help you through the basic task of comparing the boundaries so that you can convert the election statistics from the old precincts into targeting information for the newly drawn precincts.

To begin, obtain the current precinct maps and those for the past two elections. In many cases, what appears to be a complicated boundary adjustment may not be. Occasionally you will find that the lines have remained the same and only the numbers of the precinct have changed. Or large precincts may have been split in half with the overall boundaries of the two new ones being identical to the old single precinct.

Next, create a precinct conversion table like the one below, which relates the old precincts to the current one:

SAMPLE PRECINCT CONVERSION TABLE

Old Precinct #(s)	New Precinct #(s)
6, 7	10

Place the old and the current precinct maps side by side. Some changes will be obvious, and you will be able to match these precincts easily. For example, you may find that the current precinct #10 is made up of old precincts #6 and #7. This means that when you review past election data in comparison races, you simply combine precinct data for old precincts #6 and #7 to get the data that are applicable to the current precinct #10. Go over the maps and note all simple changes on your conversion table.

Now to the problem cases. These are the shifts that you cannot trace down to the individual precinct level. For many of these areas the best approach is to arbitrarily create a large artificial precinct. For example, if the overall boundary of three old precincts closely approximates the overall boundary of two current precincts, lump these together as one artifical precinct. On the conversation table the two current precincts would have the same target rankings that would be derived from the total figures for the three old precincts.

For those few remaining precincts that you simply can't convert, you'll have to estimate past voting figures and turnout. Looking at the next largest subdivision, usually a ward, will help you. For example, you may have to assign the ward percentages to all those precincts within a ward for which you cannot get accurate conversion measurements.

Identifying Individual Voters

All of the targeting methods described above involve identifying concentrations of voters with similar characteristics who live in a certain area. This targeting gives you a priority ranking of the areas where you will conduct your voter contact programs. But even within those priority areas it is possible to further concentrate your efforts on those individuals most likely to vote. There are three techniques for identifying individual voters that you should consider in conjunction with targeting.

The most common is contacting only those individuals who are registered to vote. The electoral impact of registering new voters was a very controversial issue in the 1984 presidential campaign. The national Republican and Democratic parties and groups all across the political spectrum ran extensive voter registration drives costing millions of dollars. However, their methods are seldom applicable to low-budget state and local races. Accordingly, unless you plan an intensive effort to register new voters who will be motivated to support you, a state legislative, city council, or school board contest will usually have only a marginal effect on voter turnout.

You simply cannot count on voters registering without your direct assistance. If, as is usually the case, your resources are too limited to undertake a voter registration effort, you should limit your voter contact programs to registered voters. Lists for your voter contact programs can be compiled using only those names that appear on the list of eligible voters, which is available from the same official source as the local election returns.

In a closed primary election you will, of course, limit your voter contact programs to those who are eligible to vote in your primary. You have to assume that a state legislative or municipal race is usually not a high enough ballot priority to cause voters to change their registration, as sometimes happens in controversial statewide or national races. You do not want to waste your limited resources on voters, however supportive they may be of your candidacy, who cannot vote in your party's primary election.

Even within the group of registered voters, a further refinement is the method of identifying "historic voters." The assumption here is the same as that used in the precinct turnout measurement: those individuals who have voted regularly in past elections are the ones most likely to turn out again this year. These are the people you must reach. Historic voters are usually defined as those individuals who have voted in at least two of the past three elections. To find out who they are, voter registration lists usually have to be cross-referenced by hand with the voting records available from the county or town clerk. Remember, turnout is usually lower in a primary election. If that is the race you're running, check only the previous records for primaries to determine voting histories. For a general election race you can count both primary and general election voting.

Developing lists of historic voters can be tedious, but the results are well worth the hours you will spend in the early stages. The campaign can then concentrate its resources on those individuals who are most likely to vote on Election Day. You do not waste time, people, or money attempting to reach potential voters whose history indicates that they are not likely to vote. Especially in low turnout elections, this can be highly effective.

Concentrating on historic voters was a key component in the success of Bob Wise's 1980 race for the state senate in West Virginia. In the Democratic primary Wise defeated Senate President Bill Brotherton, a twenty-eight-year incumbent. All the pundits and professional politicians in the state were stunned by the accomplishments of this highly motivated, largely volunteer campaign. In fact, Brotherton had been considered such a definite shoe-in for reelection that the Republicans had not even fielded a candidate for the seat. This 1980 campaign for elective office was Wise's first, but he brought to it his extensive organizing experience as the director of a statewide tax reform group, FEAT (Fair & Equitable Assessment of Taxes). Knowing he faced an uphill battle on name recognition and would be seriously outspent by his opponent, Wise focused all of his campaign resources on the historic primary voters in his district. He concentrated his personal door-to-door visits in those counties that targeting showed to have the highest persuadability and used volunteer phone banks in the counties with a lower priority ranking. While Brotherton's media spots played to the greater Charleston area, the Wise campaign quietly made three to four contacts each with those voters who could provide the margin for their upset victory. Wise's meteoric rise was repeated in 1982 when he used the same campaign tactics to beat out a crowded field to win the congressional seat from West Virginia's 3rd District.

Conclusion

In these first two chapters we have concentrated on defining your message and your campaign's target audience. These are the two crucial elements of a winning campaign strategy, the necessary foundation for all of the techniques that follow. Later, we will lay out in detail a variety of methods to deliver your message to your target audience. There will be lots of information about each delivery mechanism and the resources needed to reach voters most effectively. But as you work through the details, keep the big picture clearly in mind: winning depends on repetitive, persuasive communication with your likely supporters.

3

CAMPAIGN PLANNING AND MANAGEMENT

Everyone knows at least one story of a candidate who won completely by surprise—a fluke that can only be chalked up to a personality quirk, a scandal, or a party landslide. But in almost all other instances, the victory goes to the well-organized campaign that communicates a clear message to a carefully targeted audience in an efficient and effective manner. We've already talked about crafting your message and targeting your audience. Now, what's the secret to developing efficient and effective campaign communications? The answer: a well-thought-out, written plan and a penchant for organization and details. In fact, one campaign professional we know begins every staff training session with the motto "God is in the details." You may not recognize that particular religion, but the commandment is especially true in local races.

Whether your campaign is large or small, whether your budget is measured in hundreds or thousands of dollars, one of your first tasks is to draft a plan detailing how you will deliver your message to your target audience. That need should be obvious, but the truth is, if you develop a written plan for your campaign, you'll already have an edge over 80 to 90 percent of all candidates for state and local office. In fact, most local candidates start out thinking they'll shake a lot of hands, make a lot of speeches, and ride to Election Day victory on a flurry of activity—the usual campaign hoopla. To be sure, there'll be plenty of activity, but if you apply the planning techniques described here, that edge could well be your margin of victory.

Making the most effective use of limited resources is the best argument for setting out an overall campaign plan. A good written plan will also help keep you sane, serving as a road map throughout the campaign, especially in the final hectic weeks before Election Day. Methodical pursuit of the goals you've mapped out is most important when the pressure is greatest. It's too easy to get diverted into nonproductive activities. A written plan along with records that chart your progress are the easiest ways to keep the campaign on course.

A plan has one more advantage, especially for the first-time candidate. It can help inspire the confidence of potential endorsers and contributors. Think of it as though you were approaching an investor for a business loan. Having a good product idea is necessary but not sufficient. Beyond that, you would be expected to have a sound business plan that shows how you intend to carry out the idea. As a candidate, you will be asking many people to invest in you—invest their money as contributors, invest their time as staff and volunteers, and invest their own credibility as endorsers and supporters. A well-thought-out plan shows potential supporters that you are a serious candidate.

The Campaign Management Team

Before we go into the details about developing the plan, a word about staff. The best plan in the world is only as good as the individuals who carry it out. Depending on your resources, these may be paid employees or volunteers. The important thing is that the roles and responsibilites be clearly assigned.

The chief staff position in any campaign is the campaign manager. Remember the saying that a person who serves as his own lawyer has a fool for a client? Like most experienced campaigners, we firmly believe that the candidate who manages his or her own campaign is equally foolish. The candidate is the candidate. The duties involved in that role are more than a full-time job. The candidate should be contacting and persuading voters, not overseeing the day-to-day operations of the campaign staff. That responsibility must be assigned to someone else.

The campaign manager is second only to the candidate in responsibility for the success of the effort. Because this person will be making so many major decisions, the campaign manager must have the complete trust and confidence of the candidate. Good management skills are a must, as is sound political judgment. Rapport with the candidate and a good working relationship are also essential. The candidate must be kept informed, and at the same time, the campaign manager must feel that sufficient authority has been delegated to handle the job. Once the major strategy, planning, and budget decisions are made with the candidate, the campaign manager is in charge of seeing that the plan is carried out. This involves the hiring (and firing) of other key members of the campaign staff.

Any campaign is obviously a team effort. The campaign manager will need to delegate responsibility for major activities to key staff people who will make up the campaign management team. In addition to the candidate and campaign manager, these include:

FUNCTION	STAFF POSITION
Direct voter contact / Field operations	Field Coordinator
Media relations	Press Secretary
Managing candidate's schedule	Scheduler
Recruiting and managing volunteers	Volunteer Coordinator
Fundraising	Finance Coordinator
Bookkeeping/financial records	Treasurer
Compliance with election laws and reporting requirements	Attorney

The job titles may vary, but each of these functions are necessary to run a campaign. In some cases, an individual may be assigned responsibility for more than one function. In small campaigns especially, a person is likely to wear more than one hat. Or the responsibilities may be divided among several regional coordinators or assistants. In most campaigns, all the members of the campaign management team report directly to the campaign manager, who reports directly to the candidate and is the major conduit for information and ideas between the candidate and the staff. Later we will go into detail about each of these campaign activities and the staff roles necessary to carry them out.

The candidate and the campaign manager always play the major role in developing the campaign plan. The campaign's attorney should be consulted to ensure that filing and reporting deadlines are met and that all activities comply with election laws. Because their activities are an integral part of the plan, key staff members should also be involved. Close advisers to the campaign and experienced political colleagues of the candidate may also be very helpful in the initial planning.

Developing Your Campaign Plan

Every campaign activity that either delivers your message to voters or raises money or other resources is made up of many detailed steps. We'll talk about all those activities—direct voter contact, media, candidate scheduling, fundraising, recruiting and managing volunteers—with concrete "how to's" for each step. You'll see that emphasis on careful planning is repeated throughout, because each major decision in the campaign generates many specific tasks. You may, for example, decide that it is important to deliver a piece of literature about the candidate to every voting household in your targeted area three weeks before the election. This decision leads to a number of specific activities: a piece of literature must be prepared (therefore, the text, photography, and artwork must be coordinated); volunteers must be organized to distribute the literature; a distribution system must be developed and area maps prepared; and so on.

A campaign consists of thousands of similar details. Good planning allows you to anticipate most of the work and to organize tasks so that the work is carried out efficiently. At the same time you're designing each activity, you'll have to schedule it for when it will be most effective—and when it can be supported by the resources on hand.

But before you get bogged down in the specifics of each activity, let's first go through an overview of how to develop your master campaign plan.

The planning and budgeting processes in a campaign involve a series of decisions that balance the activities necessary to meet your goals with the resources available to do each job. In developing a plan for your campaign you'll have to address four fundamental questions:

- What activities will be done?

- When will they be done?

- Who will do them?

- How much will they cost?

During the planning process you will develop your own answers to these questions. As you answer each, you will develop a component of the overall plan. These components represent the manager's most important tools for coordinating and supervising all the various activities that go on simultaneously. For this reason, the plan must be a written document that can be referred to throughout the campaign.

COMPONENTS OF A CAMPAIGN PLAN

WHAT will be done?	DETAILED DESCRIPTIONS of all the activities included in the following: • The plan for direct voter contact • The media plan • The fundraising plan
WHEN will it be done?	A CAMPAIGN CALENDAR or timeline which indicates the date each activity is to be done.
WHO will do it?	A VOLUNTEER BUDGET which estimates the number of people needed for each activity.
HOW MUCH will it cost?	A MONEY BUDGET which estimates the financial costs of each activity.

Descriptions of Campaign Activities

Designing effective activities to communicate your campaign message requires making a series of policy decisions. Producing a written plan will force you to confront these questions and make conscious choices among your various options. For example, a typical voter contact activity involves distributing literature. But before you can implement that goal you will need precise answers to several questions:

- Will the literature be distributed in all precincts or only in priority areas?

- Should it go to every household, only to voters registered in your party, or only to historic voters?

- How will it be delivered—by mail or volunteers?

- When should the material reach the voters?

Answering these questions produces a specific activity description, such as: "Distribute literature door-to-door to 3,900 historic voters in precincts 2, 4, 5, 8, and 9 three weeks before the election." The campaign manager now knows how many leaflets to print and when, as well as approximately how many volunteers will be needed and the total projected costs.

Every activity should receive the same detailed treatment. If a staff is selected early enough, the campaign manager can work with each staff member to develop the descriptions for their activities, and then integrate these into an overall comprehensive plan. The specifics will vary depending on several factors, including:

- Your overall campaign strategy (i.e., What is your candidate's name recognition? How many direct contacts with targeted voters will be necessary? Will media play an important role?)

- The available resources (i.e., Will you have a small staff? Can you count on hundreds of volunteers by Election Day? Can you raise your budget early, or will fundraising be a priority activity throughout the campaign?)

- The targeting priority given to particular geographic areas or demographic groups?

But detailed descriptions are needed in *all* cases. Once you've written these they can be linked with workable timelines and budgets.

Campaign Calendar

Placing all activities on a master calendar or timeline will help you design a sequence of voter contacts that reinforce one another and build to a peak by Election Day. Make sure the dates of all your advertising buys, press conferences, and canvasses are indicated on this same calendar.

Activities that are designed to raise the necessary resources for the campaign—fundraising and volunteer recruitment—must be well underway before the activities that depend on money and people can be launched. Thus, the dates of major fundraising and recruitment efforts should also be placed on this timeline.

Plotting all these campaign activities on the same calendar will help ensure that they complement, rather than compete with, each other. For example, you want to make sure a major fundraising picnic for supporters is not scheduled on the same day that a large number of volunteers will be needed to conduct a door-to-door canvass or literature drop.

Timelines also ensure that adequate lead time is allowed for each activity. Your calendar should indicate all the stages of a particular activity. For example, it should indicate the deadlines for designing the literature, preparing walking lists and other materials, and recruiting volunteers, as well as the dates that a literature distribution is planned.

Planning Forms

The same advice applies to the calendar as to all planning forms: make it simple. Systems that are too complex are often discarded in the hectic pace of a campaign. Some managers prefer to use a giant master calendar or an easy-to-see wall chart. One simple way of doing this is to tack up 3 x 5 index cards for specific activities so that changes can be made easily. Other experienced managers use ring binders with a section for each month (or week) that contains not only the master campaign calendar, but also the more detailed plans for activities to be conducted that month. Whatever system you develop, be sure it is flexible enough to allow new information to be added and adjustments to be made.

Volunteer Budget

Most campaigns recognize the importance of budgeting money, but many fail to recognize that careful budgeting of human resources is equally vital. A well-organized volunteer force can be the single most important ingredient in helping you get your message to voters. Volunteers are, in fact, the lifeblood of small-scale campaigns. A budget for them will help you develop accurate projections of the number of people needed for each activity and plan for their most effective use.

For each activity included in your campaign plan you will need to estimate the number of volunteers and the amount of time necessary to carry it out. Beware of the fatal flaw of all beginners: unrealistic estimates. Don't assume that a handful of people can distribute literature to the whole district in one afternoon. Instead, follow a careful step-by-step process to calculate a volunteer budget for each activity. If you want to distribute 3,900 pieces of literature to historic voters in five precincts, this is how you would estimate the number of volunteers you'll need:

In a suburban district composed mostly of single-family homes, a volunteer can drop a piece of literature at an average of approximately thirty households in one hour. Remember, in this case you are contacting historic voters only, so the walking lists will indicate that certain houses on each street should be skipped. In a district with a high voter turnout you may be able to reach more households per hour. In one with low turnout, the number reached in an hour will be fewer because of the greater distances between homes. First figure out how many volunteer hours you will need.

$$\frac{3,900 \text{ households}}{30 \text{ households per hour}} = 130 \text{ volunteer hours}$$

Again, be realistic when you plan the use of the volunteers' time. Even if a volunteer is committed to working all day, you may find that seven-hour shifts are too long, especially in extreme cold or heat. If you do schedule seven-hour shifts per volunteer, remember that you may use as much as one hour of that time briefing and distributing materials to the volunteers and transporting groups to and from their assigned areas. Thus, even though the shifts are seven hours each, you would use a six-hour per person figure when calculating the volunteer budget for the drop. Now, divide the volunteer hours by the number of voter contact hours for each shift to estimate the number of volunteers that will be needed.

$$\frac{130 \text{ volunteer hours}}{6 \text{ hours per volunteer}} = 22 \text{ volunteers}$$

In addition, drivers may be needed to take volunteers to the targeted areas and to pick them up. Decide whether you will need them to stay with the groups throughout the day or only at the beginning and the end of the activity. Then budget accordingly.

As you go through this estimating process for each activity in your campaign plan, make a copy of the Volunteer & Money Budget form on page 49 and record your results as in the sample below.

DESCRIPTION OF ACTIVITY	VOLUNTEERS REQUIRED	TIME REQUIRED
Literature drop; 3,900 historic voters; precincts 2, 4, 5, 8, 9	22 volunteers @ 7 hours each; 4 drivers @ 2 hours each	1 weekend

The volunteer budget records the number of volunteers needed for each activity. The master campaign calendar indicates when they are needed. Together, these two planning tools can help you plan the recruitment program. This advance planning ensures that you will be ready to make the most effective use of volunteers.

Money Budget

The last component of the planning process is the financial plan. Because money is always limited, a money budget is necessary to allocate funds to program activities according to their priority. The budget also controls the timing of major campaign expenditures.

VOLUNTEER & MONEY BUDGET FORM

Description of Activity	Volunteers Required	Time Required	Cost

In general, careful budgeting ensures that financial decisions are made consistent with the overall campaign plan, and not on the ad hoc basis of cash on hand.

You will need to draw up two types of budgets: a program budget and a cash flow budget. Both are important management tools to be used throughout the campaign.

Program Budget

The program budget is derived by projecting expenses for each activity in the campaign plan. If you have described each activity in detail, estimating costs should not be difficult. Graphics designers or printers will give you cost estimates over the phone. You can call the post office to check on bulk postage rates. Broadcast outlets and newspapers have standard rates for political campaigns, which you can obtain from their advertising departments.

Go through the entire list of program activities detailed in your campaign plan. Estimate the cost for each. For example:

> 3,900 pieces of literature (two-sided,
> black/white, 8½ × 11, and fold) @ $.04 each = $156
> design =   50
> typesetting =   25
>
> TOTAL $231

Then record your results on the Volunteer and Money Budget Form, as in the sample below.

ACTIVITY	COST
1-pg. literature drop; 3,900 historic voters; precincts 2, 4, 5, 8, 9	$231 (design, type and print)
2-pg. letter mailed 1st class; 11,500 previous donors	$253 (postage) $287 (production)

To complete your program budget, compute any fixed costs, such as rent or staff salaries. If you plan to begin with little or no paid staff, but expand as the campaign progresses, include those projections in your budget. Unless the candidate plans to go deep into his or her own pocket during the campaign, be sure to include such personal expenses as travel and meals.

A program budget based on costs of specific activities will be much more useful in monitoring expenditures than a budget that merely sets out general estimates for categories such as printing. If your budget details how money is to be spent for specific programs, you can easily make adjustments if less is raised than you originally projected. Each of your options—such as printing fewer lawn signs, deleting a direct mail letter, or distributing fewer pieces of literature—has a specific cost that can easily be seen from the budget. Thus, spending decisions can be made that reflect the priorities of various activities.

Cash Flow Budget

The second step in developing a money budget is to determine the cash flow requirements of the campaign. To do this you need to know not only *how much* is needed for an activity but also *when* it is needed. The projections in the cash flow budget are used to determine the timing of your fundraising activities. It is important not only to raise enough money to cover the entire campaign budget, but to make sure the income in each time period is enough to pay for bills incurred during that period.

To develop a cash flow budget, go through the list of estimated expenditures for each activity in the program budget. Cross check each item with the campaign calendar to determine when the expenditure must be made. In most cases, payment will be on delivery of the material; you may even be required to put down a deposit when the order is placed because very few vendors will extend credit to political campaigns.

Record this information on a ledger sheet that indicates the monthly time periods through Election Day. For the final weeks before the election you may even want to use a weekly breakdown to provide more detailed information about the campaign's

SAMPLE CASH FLOW BUDGET

ACTIVITY	JULY	AUG.	SEPT.	OCT. 1st	OCT. 2nd	OCT. 3rd	OCT. 4th	NOV.
1 pg. literature; 3,900 copies		$231						
2-pg. direct mail; 1,150 pieces			$540					
400 lawn signs				$242				

cash flow during that critical time. List time periods horizontally across the top of the page. Down the left side of the ledger write each program activity in your campaign plan. The estimated cost of each activity should be written under the time period when the expense will be incurred. The amount of money needed to cover the planned expenses for each time period in the campaign can be determined simply by totaling all the expenditures in that column.

Optimal and Minimal Budgets

Even with the best of projections, finances never go exactly as planned. Figures will have to be adjusted constantly depending on the amount of money you're able to raise. One way to minimize adjustments and the scrambling that results is to develop contingency budgets as guidelines for campaign expenditures if more or less money becomes available.

The operating budget that you've developed covers the basic activities outlined in the campaign plan. Two other budgets should be prepared as part of the planning process: a minimal budget, which covers only bare bones necessities and identifies expenditures for the highest priority programs, to be used if only a minimal amount of money is raised; and an optimal budget for an expanded version of the original campaign plan, if more money than expected is raised. These two additional skeleton budgets provide a predetermined plan guaranteeing that major changes will be based on the campaign's priorities. If your resources expand six weeks before Election Day, what activities will you add: additional radio time; another mailing to undecided voters; a mailing to favorable voters; or a polling place handout for Election Day? How much extra money, for example, would you have to raise to run a saturation radio advertising campaign the week before Election Day? And likewise, if you do not meet your fundraising projections, which activities will you drop from your campaign plan and when? Can a press secretary be hired a month later than originally planned if fundraising goes slowly?

In the heat of the campaign it is harder to make revisions with the same care as contingency planning done in the early stages. The final weeks are not the time to make quick decisions about questions that haven't been thoroughly thought through.

Bookkeeping

Once the master plan is approved by the candidate, the campaign manager has the responsibility for overseeing the budget and approving all expenditures. A treasurer should be one of the first staff appointments made to assist with this task. In fact, in most states the name of the campaign treasurer must be indicated on all campaign literature and included in the disclaimer on all political ads. In some cases, the job entails legal responsibility for campaign debts, and should not be taken lightly.

The campaign treasurer is the person responsible for paying bills, making deposits, and keeping all the accounts and financial records of the campaign. If at all possible, assign this important job to a volunteer or staff person with accounting or bookkeeping experience. The campaign manager should be sure that an accurate bookkeeping system is set up in the beginning so the campaign leadership can closely monitor expenditures and cash flow throughout the campaign.

In some states, detailed financial reports signed by the treasurer, including copies of receipts and a record of contributions, must be filed with the state election authority. Be sure to check local campaign reporting requirements before you design your accounting system so that it will be easy to comply with reporting laws. It may help to seek the advice of a professional accountant or someone with a business background to help you do this. All financial records should be kept up to date to make it easier to determine when adjustments in the campaign plan are needed.

Making Revisions in the Campaign Plan

No campaign plan should ever be set in concrete. You will need to be flexible and make changes when they become necessary. If a new opportunity arises, you may, after careful consideration, adapt your plan to take advantage of it. If the field of candidates changes at the last minute, you may have to adjust your projections to account for it. Some changes will be last-minute reactions to the inevitable snafus that happen in every campaign whether it be the printer not delivering your literature or a sudden snow-storm that postpones your door-to-door canvass. You can't predict these, but they're easier to cope with if you have a basic plan as your foundation. If you don't panic, snafus needn't be disasters.

Other adjustments can be anticipated. To do this, establish benchmarks or milestones throughout the campaign; at these points you can review your progress and make judgments about your effectiveness in reaching certain goals. Your success in meeting fundraising goals is always one factor that will determine whether revisions must be made. Another benchmark should be volunteer recruitment. For example, if you fall behind recruiting projections you will not be able to complete all the planned volunteer work.

Throughout the campaign take the time to evaluate whether you were able to complete planned activities. Was the plan overly ambitious? Were you able, for example, to contact the number of households projected? If the estimates in your people budget are based on distributing literature to thirty households per hour and the volunteers were only able to average twenty, you will have to either limit the number of households or increase the number of volunteers.

It is also necessary to evaluate whether certain elements of your plan are working effectively. If your campaign strategy relies on getting extensive free media coverage, are you, in fact, getting that coverage? If significant amounts of candidate time have been allocated to interviews with reporters and meetings with editors that are not resulting in media coverage, you may decide to change the way the candidate's time is scheduled. Perhaps greater emphasis should be placed on direct voter contact activities.

Look also at the substance of the theme you are trying to project. Is it clearly communicated in the candidate's speeches or in the campaign's newspaper, radio, and TV coverage? If not, review your press releases. And consider how the candidate's speeches can be changed to more accurately project your message. For example, if your theme stresses responsiveness to constituents' concerns, does the format of campaign appearances allow for participation and dialogue with the candidate? Remember, all campaign communications must reinforce each other to provide repetitive, persuasive contact with voters.

The candidate and the campaign manager should reevaluate the overall plan regularly and, if necessary, revise it. Reports from members of the management team will be very useful in evaluating your progress in different areas. Don't make hasty judgments. Make improvements in the plan only when the evidence shows they're needed. Careful planning may not be as exciting as continually making crisis judgments and shooting from the hip, but it is likely that it will allow you to enjoy the most important excitement: winning.

4

SCHEDULING
THE CANDIDATE

The Scheduler

Determining the Amount of Candidate Time

The Scheduling Plan
    Voter Contact Versus Resources
    Indirect Versus Direct Communication
    The Target Audience
    Candidate's Personal Style

Scheduling Forms
    Candidate's Calendar
    Monthly Schedule
    Weekly Schedule
    Daily Schedule

Circulating Schedules

Handling Invitations
    Evaluating Requests
    Responding to Invitations
    Soliciting Invitations

Events Organized by the Campaign
    Candidate Coffees

Street Campaigning
    Crowds
    Door-to-Door Canvassing

Cancellations

Follow-Up

The candidate's time is the most precious resource in any campaign. Extremely careful planning is required to ensure that each hour of each day is well used. This chapter covers all the steps necessary to develop and carry out a scheduling plan for the candidate's activities.

Scheduling the candidate should always be one person's responsibility, that is the only way to keep track of the many details and develop a well-planned and coordinated schedule. Often, in small campaigns, the scheduler has other responsibilities, but it is best if the supervision of the schedule is not shared.

In larger campaigns, with more candidate activity, the responsibility for overseeing the details of specific events is often delegated to others, and this is usually referred to as "advance work." Advance work entails ensuring that the physical arrangements and set-up for a specific event are properly done. Sometimes advance work also involves making sure a crowd is on hand for the event.

The Scheduler

The main responsibility of the scheduler is to work closely with the campaign manager and the field and finance coordinators to allocate the candidate's time according to the targeting priorities and the campaign plan. Some of the specific duties include:

- Setting up a system to handle invitations

- Preparing the long-term calendar for candidate activity at the beginning of the campaign

- Preparing monthly and weekly schedules

- Developing a detailed daily schedule with complete information about each event

- Planning the logistics and arrangements for each event

- Distributing the candidate's schedule to campaign staff, the media, and candidate's family

Of all the people on the campaign management team, the scheduler must be someone who can handle competing demands firmly and graciously. In short, the scheduler must be someone who can say "no." The job requires firmness, patience, tact, and the ability to work well with the candidate and other members of the staff, as well as with the public.

The scheduler must also be someone who can competently handle the myriad details involved in making effective use of the candidate's time. This person is also responsible for making sure no detail is overlooked and nothing is left to chance.

Determining the Amount of Candidate Time

Before you can develop a scheduling plan you have to determine how much of the candidate's time will be available for campaign activities.

To begin, count the days from now until the election and multiply by three. Later on you will deal with hours and minutes, but initially it is useful to think in scheduling units equal to one-third of a day. Each scheduling unit—morning, afternoon, evening— lends itself to activities appropriate to that time of day.

The number of days multiplied by three gives you the gross number of units available. You will need to subtract from that figure the time the candidate requires for personal needs. This calls for a realistic assessment by the candidate. Just how much of the remainder of his or her life will stop during the campaign is an important decision?

Obviously a candidate with a full-time job will have only evenings and weekends to meet voters. For any race other than the smallest local campaign, this limited time is usually insufficient. Will the candidate be able to take a leave of absence or arrange for part-time flexible hours during the campaign.

There are also personal needs that should be considered in determining the amount of time available. What about the candidate's family obligations? How will these be juggled during the campaign? With careful planning, volunteers can assist with child care, car pool responsibilities, and the like. But there's usually no substitute for Mom or Dad at the year-end dance recital or the championship baseball game. How much time does the candidate want to reserve for family dinners or other private time away from the pace of the campaign?

There is another important personal limit on the supply of schedule time: the stamina of the candidate. How many hours a day can the candidate campaign? How late at night is the candidate willing to stay up? Personal tempo varies widely.

At one end of this scale is Peter Shapiro's first campaign for the New Jersey State Legislature in 1975. At the age of twenty-three he successfully challenged the candidate supported by the Regular Democratic Organization and became the youngest individual ever to hold that office. Shapiro's staff claims he would wear out three traveling aides some days with dawn to midnight campaigning. On a typical day he would start at 6:30 A.M. greeting voters at the commuter train stations. Then he would campaign door-to-door and attend events until nightfall. About 9:00 P.M., he would stop by two bingo games or other community events to meet voters. His day would finally end with one or two hours in the headquarters working on speeches for the following day, reviewing press releases, meeting with the campaign manager and staff, or encouraging his active corps of volunteers.

However, most candidates have less time, and certainly, less energy. In the beginning it will be virtually impossible to predict how well your candidate will hold up under the pressure of campaigning. While the scheduler who works a candidate too hard is inviting trouble, it is a waste of precious time to plan long rest periods if a candidate is "raring to go." One resolution of these conflicting pressures is to build in two or three "free" scheduling units each week. These can be held as rest periods for an exhausted candidate or used to meet last-minute scheduling demands if energy is available.

Aside from the candidate's personal needs, you must also allot enough time for internal campaign activiites such as briefings, strategy sessions, and preparation of photographs or other advertising material. Do this before you schedule time for voter contact activities. A candidate must stay informed about both current events and the campaign's progress. Allot enough time to review press coverage and reports from the campaign staff.

Likewise, there must be sufficient time to prepare for scheduled events. Major events or media appearances may require time to write or rehearse a speech or to study an issue in depth. Preparation is vital if the candidate is to get the most from an appearance.

Also, schedule time for your candidate to make phone calls and hold meetings with key people and contributors. Time is also needed to write personal notes and thank-yous. Work closely with the finance coordinator to be sure that this important personal contact and follow up is not overlooked. Jimmy Carter made this style of campaigning famous when his birthday note to the wife of a Democratic county chairman made national news during the 1976 Iowa caucuses. Successful local candidates have always known the value of a personal approach.

Once you calculate the time required for personal needs and internal campaign tasks, subtract that from the original total to get the number of units your candidate has available for other campaign activities.

The Scheduling Plan

Developing a schedule consistent with your overall campaign strategy is the only way to avoid haphazard, poorly targeted use of the candidate's time. Several factors should be considered by the campaign manager and scheduler in developing this plan:

- Amount of time spent on voter contact versus raising campaign resources

- Indirect versus direct communication with voters

- The target audience for candidate contacts

- Personal style of the candidate

Because their activities will be affected, it is best to involve the field director, press secretary, and finance coordinator in the scheduling plan.

Voter Contact Versus Resources

The first decision you face is how to divide your candidate's time between contacting potential voters and raising the necessary resources for the campaign. Many hours of candidate time in any campaign will have to be devoted to individual meetings with donors, fundraising events, and efforts to recruit volunteers. These resources are essential in the overall campaign effort to reach voters, but it is important that an appropriate balance be struck.

The balance between these demands will vary in different campaigns, but as a general rule the candidate should spend as much time as possible contacting voters. Others may be as effective with fundraising, but no one else can say, "I'm running for office. Please vote for me." Many of the techniques described in this book—for example, establishing a Finance Committee to increase the number of people to solicit contributions—will help you minimize the amount of candidate time spent on raising resources.

Indirect Versus Direct Communication

In the earliest planning stages, a strategic decision should be made about whether the campaign is capable of generating significant amounts of press coverage and how valuable that coverage will be. These decisions determine how much candidate time should be allocated to interviews, press conferences, and media-related events as opposed to direct contact with voters.

In a large district where it is impossible for the candidate to reach all the voters in person, and where the media are likely to cover local campaigns, the design for the candidate's time would likely emphasize mediated communication with voters. Conversely, if direct communications with potential voters is essential to winning, as is most often the case in a small district, then the candidate would be better off talking to potential voters than to reporters. Again, the word here is balance.

Timing is also important. Is press coverage crucial to establishing early name recognition and building the credibility of your candidate? Or does your strategy depend on first building the campaign's momentum through direct contact with voters, both by the candidate and volunteers? (The latter may be a factor if you intend to catch a longtime incumbent off guard.) These and similar questions must be answered when deciding what role events designed to get press coverage should play in the scheduling plan.

The Target Audience

Before you can decide where the candidate's time should be spent, you must know where the critical persuadable voters are, where your likely base of favorable voters is located, and which, if any, areas should be written off as hopeless. The priority ranking of geographic areas produced by percent-of-effort targeting should be your primary basis for allocating units of the candidate's time. Precinct targeting will give you an even more precise analysis of the areas in your district. The raw numbers should, of course, be modified by the importance placed on specific interest groups or constituencies in the campaign's overall strategy. These targeting priorities should always be kept in mind when accepting and generating invitations.

Candidate's Personal Style

An understanding of the candidate's strengths and weaknesses will be essential to developing your scheduling plan. For example:

- Is the candidate an effective speaker at large events or are smaller, more informal settings better?
- Does campaigning in crowds pose a problem?
- Will the candidate do well in debate situations?

Similarly, consider the strengths and weaknesses of your opponent. In a recent Rhode Island city council race one candidate discovered that her opponent could be his own worse enemy in certain campaign situations: he became flustered, angry, and abusive during debates. The candidate not only encouraged this format whenever possible, but her press secretary worked to get media coverage of each event. On the other hand, if your opponent is a charismatic orator while your candidate comes across more effectively in smaller settings, try to avoid large audience situations that invite comparison.

Scheduling Forms

Once you have determined the amount of candidate time available and established the guidelines for allocating time, you are ready to begin developing schedules. There are four forms to help you keep track of the candidate's time: the candidate's master calendar, the monthly schedule, the weekly schedule, and the daily schedule. These forms provide a range of scheduling perspectives from a general overview of all major blocks of time until the election, to a detailed account of the activities in a single day. The following section reviews each of these and provides a sample you can duplicate for your own use.

Candidate's Calendar

The campaign manager is responsible for maintaining the master calendar or timeline on which is listed all campaign activities and deadlines. The candidate's calendar described here covers only the candidate's activities. Obviously, close coordination is required to keep these two up to date.

Prepare a calendar to give you an overview of important dates and scheduling opportunities for the entire campaign period. Begin by entering these items:

- Important dates and deadlines in the campaign, such as the candidate's announcement, and primary and Election Days

- The deadlines for producing any media spots that will involve the candidate

- Commitments that have already been made for candidate appearances

- Dates of major events that should be included in the candidate's schedule, such as fairs, political conventions, and candidate forums. (Make note of those events for which an invitation needs to be solicited.)

CANDIDATE'S MASTER CALENDAR

Month: _____	Month: _____	Month: _____
1st week	1st week	1st week
2nd week	2nd week	2nd week
3rd week	3rd week	3rd week
4th week	4th week	4th week

Month: _____	Month: _____	Month: _____
1st week	1st week	1st week
2nd week	2nd week	2nd week
3rd week	3rd week	3rd week
4th week	4th week	4th week

Month: _____	Month: _____	Month: _____
1st week	1st week	1st week
2nd week	2nd week	2nd week
3rd week	3rd week	3rd week
4th week	4th week	4th week

The candidate's calendar is also used to allocate time to specific target geographic areas and interest groups. For example, you should divide the total time the candidate spends on door-to-door canvassing according to the targeting percentages for each area. On the candidate's calendar, block out the corresponding number of time units to be spent in each area.

As you continue to fill in the calendar throughout the campaign, you will be able to monitor how closely the use of candidate time reflects the priorities of the scheduling plan. This monitoring is very important. Mounting pressure from people inside and outside the campaign to accept "must" invitations tends to wreak havoc with the priorities set out in the campaign plan.

Use the candidate's calendar to ensure that the activities build gradually, peaking for maximum effectiveness just before Election Day. This principle is essential throughout the campaign since voters are most attentive just before they vote. To build momentum, the scheduler must coordinate increased candidate activities with other advertising, visibility efforts, and field operations of the campaign.

Monthly Schedule

The next step is to begin refining the candidate's calendar by preparing expanded monthly schedules. Begin about four weeks in advance by transferring all major commitments listed on the candidate's calendar. Work with the field director to confirm the times the candidate will be canvassing door-to-door. Also, work with the press secretary to allot time for interviews, news conferences, and other media appearances. Include any campaign fundraising events that will involve the candidate.

Once this time is blocked out and you know the general areas where the candidate is scheduled to be, you can begin soliciting additional invitations or developing plans for campaign-generated events. Be sure the necessary time for campaign organizational meetings, contacts with donors, and phone calls is included in the monthly schedule.

Monthly schedules need not include detailed information, so a form that allows one box per day for notes should be sufficient. You can make your own or take the sample on page 67 and enlarge it.

CAMPAIGN MONTHLY SCHEDULE

Campaign _____ Month: _____ Year: _____

HDQS: _____

SUN	MON	TUES	WED	THUR	FRI	SAT

Weekly Schedule

A more detailed schedule prepared one week in advance is the third step in planning the candidate's time. At this stage, you should be working in half-hour segments. This is the time to consider last-minute invitations and invitations that may have been put on hold. The weekly schedule should include travel and preparation time, meals, and personal obligations.

If you use the sample on page 69, photocopy the days onto a legal-size sheet so you can see the whole week at a glance.

Daily Schedule

The last step is the detailed daily schedule, the final blueprint that accounts for every minute of the candidate's time and includes complete information about every event. For each event the daily schedule should note:

- Precise location of event

- Name of sponsoring organization or host

- Exact time of the event and when the candidate is expected to arrive and leave

- Format of the event: what will be required of the candidate— informal handshaking, speech (how long?), question-and-answer period

- Estimated attendance at the event

- Contact person for the event, including home and office phone numbers should any last-minute communications be necessary

- Time required to get from one stop to another

- Staff or volunteer aide assigned to attend with the candidate

The daily schedule is the test of a good scheduler. How complete and accurate the details are and how well the timing has been estimated will determine how smoothly the candidate's day

CAMPAIGN WEEKLY SCHEDULE

Week of _____ to _____

DAY _____	DATE _____
8	00
	30
9	00
	30
10	00
	30
11	00
	30
12	00
	30
1	00
	30
2	00
	30
3	00
	30
4	00
	30
5	00
	30
6	00
	30
7	00
	30
8	00
	30
9	00
	30

DAY _____	DATE _____
8	00
	30
9	00
	30
10	00
	30
11	00
	30
12	00
	30
1	00
	30
2	00
	30
3	00
	30
4	00
	30
5	00
	30
6	00
	30
7	00
	30
8	00
	30
9	00
	30

DAY _____	DATE _____
8	00
	30
9	00
	30
10	00
	30
11	00
	30
12	00
	30
1	00
	30
2	00
	30
3	00
	30
4	00
	30
5	00
	30
6	00
	30
7	00
	30
8	00
	30
9	00
	30

will run. Don't guess. If you don't know how long it will take to drive from headquarters to the Holiday Inn, time it yourself or have someone else do it and report the result to you. Depending on the time of an event, should you adjust for rush hour traffic? Is there road construction that necessitates finding an alternate route? What about parking? Where is it located? If it is far away how much time should you include for parking, or do you plan to have the aide drop the candidate at the door?

These are just a few examples of the numerous details the scheduler must anticipate. Many are the tales of woe about schedules gone awry that begin with, "But I assumed. . . ." A cardinal rule we learned doing advance for a presidential candidate, which holds equally well for all campaigns: "Assumption is the mother of all screw-ups."

Use the sample daily schedule on page 71 as a model in developing your own. Keep the checklist above handy to ensure that each point is covered for each scheduled event.

Circulating Schedules

Key people in the campaign must be kept informed about the candidate's activities. Make a distribution list and see to it that the appropriate people receive copies of all the schedules. Be sure these key people receive weekly and daily schedules several days in advance of the dates they cover. The daily schedule should also be posted in the headquarters and made available to the candidate's family so they can easily locate the candidate if necessary.

Prepare a version of the weekly schedule for interested media, listing only those candidate activities that are open to the press. Do not include personal time, campaign strategy meetings, or private meetings with contributors or key supporters on this copy unless for some reason you want to call one of these to the attention of the press. Be sure to note any special arrangements that have been made for press coverage at each event. These schedules should be released by the campaign press secretary early enough to attract media coverage.

Prior to the start of each day of campaigning, the scheduler should go over the detailed schedule with the candidate. This is a perfect opportunity to review the key elements of each event as well as answer any questions the candidate may have. Hold the meeting the first thing in the morning or at the end of the previous day. This will allow enough time for last-minute changes and for filling in data that might have been overlooked. Once the candi-

SAMPLE DAILY SCHEDULE

Daily Schedule—Wednesday, September 11

6:15 a.m.	Picked up at home by aide/driver Bill Parkman.
6:30 a.m.	Arrive Parkinson Instruments Factory, North Gate, 1220 State St.
	Accompanied by John Ross, I.A.M. Local 19, business representative, and Susan Stewart, campaign volunteer. Distribute literature and handshaking with workers during 6:30-6:50 shift change.
6:50 a.m.	Depart Parkinson.
7:00 a.m.	Arrive commuter train terminal at corner Regent St. and Main, accompanied by Susan Stewart. Handshaking with commuters.
7:45 a.m.	Depart commuter terminal.
8:00 a.m.	Meeting Calvert Cafe, 2035 Calvert St., #462-6335. (Cafe owner is Richard Wallace. Has contributed $60 to compaign.)
	Breakfast with John Ross, Eleanor Norton, William Taylor, Bill Sterns—members of campaign Finance Committee. Purpose: To discuss fundraising plan for small business owners in district.
9:20 a.m.	Depart Calvert Cafe.
9:40 a.m.	Arrive campaign headquarters.
	Meeting with campaign manager and media coordinator to discuss radio publicity.
10:30 a.m.	Meeting with leaders of Southeast Community Organization. Elizabeth Hollander, pres.; James Delgado, vice-pres.; Rita Juarez, treasurer; Frank Horton, staff director. Discussion of problems in Southeast neighborhood. S.C.O.'s candidate endorsement will be decided by their Executive Committee at their Sept. 22 meeting.
11:40 a.m.	Depart for Holiday Inn.
12:00 p.m.	Arrive luncheon Holiday Inn, 1280 Westview Ave., #863-4802.
	Wiltshire Room—luncheon sponsored by city-wide PTA. Approximately 100 PTA officers will attend. Introductions by Mrs. Selma Taylor, president. Two speakers—yourself and John Burlington, Republican State Senate candidate. Remarks 10-15 minutes, followed by Q & A.
	Local press will attend.
1:30 p.m.	Depart for business office. Afternoon at work. Followed by family dinner at home.
7:10 p.m.	Picked up at home by aide/driver Roberta Schur.
7:20 p.m.	Arrive at candidate coffee. Home of Michael and Jane Rollins, 735 Sutter St., #386-3044. Approximately 45 people present. Introductions and follow-up pitch will be made by Jane Rollins. Remarks 5-10 minutes, followed by Q & A for 10 minutes.
8:10 p.m.	Depart coffee.
8:30 p.m.	Stop by bingo game at St. Stephens, 470 Columbus St. West entrance. Approximately 200 seniors from precincts 3 and 4 attend.
9:00 p.m.	Depart bingo. Return home.

date is on the road, further schedule changes are nearly impossible.

A copy of the daily schedule should also be given to the driver or aide who will accompany the candidate. Attach precise instructions for the travel route, where to park, and which entrance to use. Add any maps that may be needed. As a backup, give the aide an extra copy of the candidate's speech or other important materials. The aide can also be given additional background or briefing material to hand to the candidate at the appropriate time. This information fits best on 3 × 5 index cards that the candidate can review and then store easily in a pocket or purse.

Developing Schedules

There are three major building blocks for developing the candidate's schedule:

- Setting up a system to handle invitations

- Creating campaign events

- Arranging informal street campaigning

Handling Invitations

Before you start creating opportunities for your candidate to meet voters, look at what others have arranged for you. These may include such political events as candidate forums, meetings of groups with an interest in public affairs, and nonpolitical gatherings where the candidate can contact important constituent groups.

Unsolicited invitations will begin to flow in from the beginning of the campaign. It is the scheduler's job (in consultation with the candidate and the campaign manager) to judge each event's value for voter persuasion and media coverage and then to decide whether the candidate should attend.

Evaluating Requests

You will find that a standard form, such as the one below, is useful for recording all invitations. It helps you understand quickly the

SCHEDULING REQUEST FORM

Date of Request _____   Accept _____

Decision made _____   Reject _____

Date of Response _____   Hold _____

Event _____

Date _____ Time Begins _____

Location _____

Number Expected to Attend _____ Will There Be Media Present? _____

Sponsoring Organization _____

Address _____ Phone _____

Contact Person _____

Address _____ Phone (Office) _____

_____ Phone (Home) _____

Description of Program _____

Nature of Candidate's Presentation _____

Questions & Answers? _____

Who Will Introduce the Candidate? _____

How Long Is Candidate to Speak? _____ Topic Preference _____

Other Speakers _____

OK to Send Surrogate? _____

Distribute Literature? _____

Other Information _____

_____

_____

_____

key facts about an invitation, assess its value, and record decisions made and action taken.

The scheduling request form assures that the same data is obtained about each proposed event and makes it easier to circulate the request to the candidate and other campaign staff for a decision about attending. Especially if you do not receive a written invitation, the form ensures that important information is not omitted in dealing with telephone invitations.

Record detailed information about the event, including:

- The name, address, and phone number of the person extending the invitation. If different persons are to be contacted to make arrangements, list this information, too.

- The name and a description of the sponsoring group.

- The day of the week, date, and time of the event.

- The location of the event—both the street address and the political subdivision (precinct, ward, etc.). Include detailed travel directions.

- Approximate number of people expected to attend.

- The format of the program (speech, debate, reception, etc.).

- When in the program is the candidate's presence necessary?

- Will the candidate make a formal speech or informal remarks? How long? Will there be a question and answer period?

- Who will introduce the candidate?

- Will there be other speakers? If so, who?

- Type of press coverage expected.

- Deadline for responding.

- If the candidate cannot attend, is it possible to send a surrogate? Or to send a message to the group?

Though it is not reasonable to expect that initial invitations will answer every question, all this information must be checked thoroughly before a final decision is made on any event. Leave nothing to chance.

Once an invitation is accepted the same form can be used to record additional information that will be used in preparing the daily schedule and the candidate's briefing materials.

Such information might include:

- The name of a campaign supporter or friendly contact within the group who can be a resource person.

- Any special information that may be helpful in preparing remarks. What are the key concerns or major issues of the group? Are there special subjects to avoid or include?

- Names of influential people the candidate is likely to meet. Background information on individuals the candidate does not know is very helpful.

- The arrangements for distributing campaign literature at the event.

Responding to Invitations

The first rule is no one, including the candidate, should accept any invitation without careful evaluation. In the middle of campaigning it's tempting to quickly say yes to a friendly request. When that happens, carefully planned schedules go out the window. Everyone should be taught a standard response along the lines of: "I'm sure the candidate would love to attend, but I'll have to check with the campaign scheduler to see what commitments have been made." All invitations should be referred to the scheduler.

A second rule is always respond to invitations in writing. This is by far the best way to avoid misunderstandings. Even if an invitation is accepted or rejected orally, a follow-up confirmation letter should be sent.

You can simplify your work by preparing several form letters with a variety of standard responses. As the pace of the campaign accelerates, an overworked scheduler can ask clerical volunteers to substitute particulars from the invitation into a form reply. The following five responses almost cover the waterfront:

- Acceptance

- Regrets; other commitments

- Ask for more information

- Candidate cannot attend; will send surrogate if that is all right

- Invitation extended too far in advance; please contact later

If you are declining an invitation, reply as promptly as possible to allow the organization time to make other arrangements. A scheduler seldom makes friends in a campaign, but can avoid making unnecessary enemies.

Saying "no" is an art. The letter should politely state that the candidate is unavailable and sincerely regrets being unable to attend. Express a continued interest in the organization, its meetings, or its issues. It is usually best to have the letter signed by the scheduler or campaign manager so the candidate is not associated with the refusal.

If the occasion warrants it, consider asking if a surrogate speaker or campaign supporter may attend in the candidate's place. Or would it be appropriate for the candidate to send a message to the group? If a key campaign supporter holds a position within the organization, take the time for a phone call to personally convey the candidate's regrets. Ask if you can make literature or other campaign materials available to the meeting.

In making scheduling decisions, it is important to distinguish between one-time and recurring events. Suppose an invitation to address the local League of Women Voters' monthly meeting conflicts with another organization's annual convention. If both groups are important, accept the annual convention, since it is your only opportunity to meet that group during the campaign period, but try to work with the League to reschedule the candidate's appearance at a later meeting.

Beware of making commitments too far in advance. As Election Day draws nearer it becomes harder to predict the needs of the campaign. Especially in the final weeks, scheduling demands a great deal of flexibility. If you receive an invitation for an event that is months away, you can reply that you cannot yet confirm whether the candidate will be available. Keep the invitation on file, make a note on the candidate's calendar, and contact the sponsors as the event draws closer.

Soliciting Invitations

As the scheduler begins to fill in the candidate's calendar with events to which the candidate has been invited and will be attending, imbalances are likely to appear. Unsolicited invitations will probably give the candidate access to only a few of the audiences targeted in the campaign strategy. The second and more challenging part of the scheduler's job entails soliciting politically valuable invitations to events that will provide voter contact and media attention in areas that are high priorities in the campaign plan.

The first step is to identify regular meetings, special events, and places where crowds of voters gather in targeted areas. Check with local Chambers of Commerce; read community calendars and newspapers; call local unions, neighborhood organizations, civic, fraternal, and service groups. Contact all the political organizations that make candidate endorsements. Ask supporters about events or meetings in their neighborhoods. Supporters who belong to key organizations may also suggest scheduling possibilities. Persons who have been responsible for scheduling in previous campaigns should also be asked for their ideas.

At the same time, collect information about places in targeted neighborhoods where potential voters congregate, such as business and shopping areas, bus or subway stops. Who are the major employers in the area? What are their policies about meeting workers at plant gates or in the lunchroom? This type of information will help you schedule informal handshaking/walking tours.

Once you have done this research you can begin soliciting invitations. Ask supporters and friends or family of the candidate to contact organizations with which they are affiliated. Even if you have no inside contact, do not hesitate to approach a group that would be valuable. The worst they can do is say "no." If you are flexible about both time and format, most will be receptive.

Don't get locked into thinking that an event can't be worthwhile unless the candidate makes a speech. Especially in the early stages of a local campaign, it may be just as helpful to have a staunch supporter personally introduce the candidate to members of an organization at a dinner or reception. We know one perennially successful candidate in a rural Nebraska community who wouldn't think of missing a funeral. The same holds true for many a Boston politician and wakes.

Also, don't limit yourself to large events. If the candidate is meeting people who may volunteer or who influence other voters, a small informal gathering can be just as valuable as a large, more impersonal event. In deciding where to send the candidate, consider both the quality of voter contact at the event and the number of voters the event can reach, either directly or through media coverage.

In addition to scheduling voter contact activities in targeted geographic areas, look for scheduling opportunities that help convey the major themes of the campaign. A well-chosen media event can help voters identify the candidate with the major positions that make up the campaign message. For example, if problems of the elderly are a major concern, identify group meetings and senior citizens' centers with regular meal or social programs where the candidate might speak or do informal campaigning. Events that can gain media attention demonstrating the candidate's concern for seniors will further reinforce your campaign message.

Events Organized by the Campaign

Thus far, we have emphasized events planned and organized by groups in the community to which the candidate is invited as a speaker or guest. In local campaigns it is essential to take advantage of these invitations because they give the candidate valuable exposure without requiring a great deal of staff time. Events organized by the campaign involve much more work but they are often necessary to meet your voter contact, volunteer recruitment, and fundraising goals.

Candidate Coffees

The most common type of campaign organized events are small, informal gatherings held in supporters' homes, often called house parties or candidate coffees. If carefully targeted to priority areas, candidate coffees are an effective way of persuading undecided voters. They are usually small enough to allow for direct contact with the candidate. Perhaps their greatest value is in motivating people to volunteer time and donate money.

A candidate can make as many as two or three coffees in an evening if the timing is carefully planned. This is a very effective use of time and multiplies the candidate's exposure to voters. One testimony to the value of candidate coffees comes from the National Conservative Political Action Committee: "The number of coffees your candidate attends should be limited only by the strength of his kidneys."

You should recruit one of your most capable volunteers to oversee the entire candidate coffee program. The coffee coordinator is responsible for organizing the coffees but must confirm the candidate's availability with the scheduler before dates and times are finalized. The coffee coordinator must oversee all details: recruiting hosts and hostesses, distributing materials, regularly checking the process of invitations and calls, scheduling someone to make the "pitch" at each coffee, and collecting lists, pledge cards, and contributions after each coffee.

To get a series of candidate coffees going, establish a system that pyramids. You can start with a coffee held by key supporters from areas you have targeted. Ask each guest to duplicate the event in his or her own neighborhood. To continue expanding the pyramid, the giver of each successive coffee should attempt to recruit at least two new people to hold coffees in their homes. Precinct coordinators and others in the campaign field organization should also be encouraged to recruit people to hold coffees in target areas.

Written invitations should be sent out ten days before the candidate coffee. These can be personal notes giving the candidate's name, the office sought, and where and when the coffee will be held; or the campaign can provide printed invitations on which the sponsor of the event adds time and place. Always ask for an RSVP.

It is usually necessary to send about three times as many invitations as the number of guests you can handle. Invitations should be aimed at undecideds and potential supporters. Avoid the temptation to build easy crowds by only inviting people who already support the campaign. Unless you reach new people, there is little gain from the time invested.

The key to success is to follow up each invitation with a telephone call two or three days before the coffee. Whether made by the host or hostess or by a campaign volunteer, these personal reminders will greatly increase your turnout. In this call you can also encourage guests to bring their friends.

As guests arrive, be sure they sign an attendance sheet. You'll need names, addresses, and telephone numbers to follow up after the coffee. Have candidate literature and other campaign materials available at the same table. Name tags are helpful if the people attending the coffee do not know one another. They also help a candidate refer to the guests by name.

The candidate should arrive about thirty minutes after the start of the coffee. At a small gathering the candidate can be personally introduced to each guest; at larger gatherings the host or hostess can make the introduction to the group. The format should be informal. The candidate should only speak for five to ten minutes and answer questions from the group for another fifteen to twenty.

The host or hostess should then diplomatically wind up the questions, stating that the candidate has to leave for another campaign engagement. It is very important for the candidate to be brief and leave at a high point in the meeting.

Now comes the "pitch." It must be dynamic and persuasive. If the candidate has motivated people, you want to translate that motivation into usable campaign resources. Choose someone who is a good speaker, possibly the host or hostess, the finance coordinator, or a strong supporter. Explain that the guests can play a vital role in the candidate's election. Describe the campaign and the kind of help that is needed. Urge them to volunteer time; ask them to donate money. Tell them to whom to make out the checks.

Don't hurry. Most pitches fail because they end too quickly leaving guests feeling no immediate pressure to contribute. Try to get as many people as possible to commit themselves at the meeting.

Thank each person individually as you collect the pledge cards and contributions. See if anyone has any unanswered questions that warrant a follow-up phone call or letter.

Judge the success of your candidate coffee not only by the number of voters who attend, but also by how many volunteers you recruit and how much money you raise. The coffee coordinator should collect pledge cards and contributions after each event and assure that appropriate follow-up is done by the campaign.

New volunteers should receive a call within two days enlisting them for a specific activity. Contributors should receive a thank-you letter signed by the candidate. Most important, the host or hostess and organizer of the coffee should receive a special word of thanks.

Street Campaigning

All of the activities discussed so far involve the candidate contacting voters at events. This section covers candidate contact with voters where they naturally gather and in their homes. This "street campaigning" is an essential part of any campaign. One candidate told us we should refer to this as the "shoe leather" section. In fact, one successful candidate for state representative in Oregon told friends that she measured progress in her first campaign by the number of times she had her favorite walking shoes resoled.

Crowds

Campaigning in crowds can be effective if your strategy calls for a high visibility effort. Especially in small communities, it can dramatically increase candidate name recognition.

Informal walking tours and campaigning where people gather provide opportunities to meet large numbers of voters in a short period of time. It takes careful research to determine what areas have natural crowd concentrations, and what are the times and days that allow the candidate the best access to your targeted voters. Don't rely on guesswork. Check out each location personally at the suggested times before you place it on the candidate's schedule. The better you know your district, the more creative you will be in locating good campaigning sites, such as neighborhood shopping areas, sporting events, fairs, and festivals.

Other possibilities for contacting voters include major train, subway, or bus stops in targeted neighborhoods. It's usually best to campaign among commuters during the morning rush hours, while they are waiting for transportation. In the evening they will rapidly pass you by on their way home.

When the candidate is working crowds, the campaign effort should be highly visible to attract attention and aid name recognition. The candidate should be prominently identified and accompanied by volunteers with signs who will steer passersby to him or her to shake hands. Volunteers passing out literature should also have an ample supply of pledge cards or fundraising reply envelopes to get the names of anyone who expresses support for the candidate.

Be sure to check legal regulations and obtain permission before campaigning on private property. Another often overlooked bit of public relations: pick up all discarded campaign literature before you leave.

To campaign at plant gates, obtain permission and make arrangements in advance with the company's management, and with the union representative if the plant is organized. Obtain information about the shift change to determine when the greatest number of employees will be going into the plant. Try to campaign at the beginning of each shift—your material is more likely to be read at that time than when workers are hurrying home. If possible, get a prominent labor official or union member who is a supporter to campaign with the candidate. Volunteers with signs should distribute literature while the candidate shakes hands and greets each worker.

Door-to-Door Canvassing

Going door-to-door to meet voters is one of the most effective ways to establish the personal contact with voters that is so important in local campaigns. Candidate canvassing is a significant investment of time and energy, but the payoff is well worth it. Often this is the single largest block of the candidate's time. The field coordinator will select the areas and the specific homes the candidate will visit as determined by targeting priorities. The scheduler's job is to coordinate these assignments with the rest of the schedule. Remember, you want to minimize wear and tear on the candidate. If he or she will be canvassing on the west side in the afternoon, schedule the rest of the day's events nearby to decrease travel time.

Before canvassing a new area the candidate should be well briefed on neighborhood problems. It is important to take the time to talk with people and to listen to the issues that concern them, but avoid long conversations or going into people's houses. Anyone interested in talking at length should be invited to a candidate coffee.

Everyone who responds favorably should be asked to sign a pledge card and become involved in the campaign. Be sure the volunteer coordinator follows up and that these names are added to the lists for fundraising events.

Leave a piece of campaign literature with each person you visit. If no one is home, leave a note in the door: "I'm sorry you weren't home when I stopped by on Thursday. . . . " It can really slow you down to write these as you go along, so one technique is to have them prepared in advance by volunteers. A warning: never leave literature in the mailbox. It is illegal to put anything in a mailbox that has not been stamped and sent through the postal service.

Remember the value of repetitive, persuasive communication with your likely supporters. Door-to-door canvassing by the candidate is most effective when it is reinforced by other campaign activities. For example, a few days before the candidate's visit, volunteers can leave literature and a note at each home to be visited, indicating that the candidate will soon be calling on them. A candidate canvass can also be followed up by a letter (either mailed or delivered by volunteers) thanking favorable voters for their support and enclosing additional material for those who are still undecided.

Cancellations

One of the most difficult tasks for a scheduler is canceling an appearance by the candidate. Obviously, the closer to the time of the event, the harder cancellations are for everyone involved. Try to avoid canceling if you possibly can. If it's done too often the campaign and the candidate will soon gain the reputation for being hopelessly disorganized.

Careful scheduling will help you minimize the possibility, but sometimes a cancellation or a postponement is a necessity. The host or sponsoring organization will never be happy with the change, but be as diplomatic as possible. Explain the reasons honestly. Let them know you understand the problems it creates, but that it's unavoidable. If possible, offer to reschedule the candidate at a later date. Your major goal is to avoid making enemies for the candidate.

Follow-Up

Events are not done for their own sake; their value is in voter contact, volunteer recruitment, and fundraising. Much of that value can be lost unless careful attention is paid to the follow-up of an event. The scheduler should work with the field coordinator and the volunteer coordinator to ensure this is done. Be sure voters who have requested material or information receive a prompt reply from the campaign. Remember to call the next day to confirm volunteer commitments and to send thank-you letters to contributors. These final details maximize the effectiveness of the candidate's time.

5

DIRECT CONTACT WITH VOTERS: FIELD ORGANIZATIONS

The Field Coordinator

The Voter Contact Plan

Identifying Voters

The Door-to-Door Canvass
Preparing Materials for the Canvass
Recruiting and Training Volunteers
Recordkeeping and Follow-Up

Canvassing by Telephone

Print Communication with Voters
Campaign Leaflets
Direct Mail

Voter Contact Through Groups

Get Out the Vote (GOTV)

Absentee Voting

Voter Registration

As we keep saying, repetitive, persuasive communication with likely supporters is the key to winning elections at any level. But unlike major statewide or national contests where personal contact with the majority of voters is impossible, a local campaign can often communicate directly with every member of its target audience. In fact, the winning candidate in a local race will almost always be the person who has done the best job of contacting voters individually.

One-to-one communication initiated by the candidate or campaign volunteers is the fundamental way your message will be delivered. News coverage and advertising can help reinforce your message, but personal communications delivered by your field organization are critical.

Depending on the stage of the campaign, direct voter contact activities may serve a variety of functions. In the initial stages your goal will be to determine which individuals are likely to vote and who they favor. By identifying these "Favorable," "Persuadable," and "Unfavorable" voters early on, the campaign can tailor its future communications to each target audience. People who say that they support your candidate can be asked to volunteer or contribute money. Voters with no preference can be asked why and offered your arguments.

No further action should be taken toward voters identified as unfavorable to your candidate. The best thing that can happen is for them to forget about the race until after Election Day. Do not delude yourself into believing that more than a small percentage of your opponent's supporters can be won over. An intensive effort will waste resources and result in frustration for you and more voters for your opponent. Remember, your goal is to build a winning margin of voters, it's not to convert the entire population of your district.

The Field Coordinator

The field coordinator is the staff person responsible for coordinating all facets of the voter contact program. If your campaign plan depends on extensive direct contact with voters this is obviously a very important position.

Choose an individual with good technical and human relations skills who can handle a host of details and people simultaneously. Individuals who have run door-to-door canvass operations for local charities or citizens' groups often have the right background, as may people with management experience in the direct selling business.

The field organization is usually the campaign's major consumer of volunteer time. Efficient coordination is critical since there will rarely be enough people available to complete all the possible tasks. Every volunteer must have a specific job to perform, the materials to do it effectively, and adequate training and supervision.

There will be roles in the field organization for volunteers with all levels of skills and time commitments. Most important are those willing to canvass door-to-door or conduct other forms of street campaigning. But there's also work to be done in the campaign office or even volunteers' homes. Among the tasks that must be completed are transcribing voting lists, compiling phone numbers, addressing and mailing letters, and maintaining records.

In a well-staffed campaign, the field coordinator can assign responsibility for such functions as list preparation, recordkeeping, and telephone follow-up to specific individuals. Middle-management of the field operation is usually best broken down geographically. Regional field coordinators should supervise voter contact and follow-up in the major areas of the district. Under each regional coordinator may be several community coordinators who handle a small town or urban precinct. When such a pyramid style structure is used, reporting and supervisory duties must be clearly defined to avoid overlap and conflict.

One key specialist on the field staff will be the person in charge of Election Day activities. Since planning for the Get Out the Vote (GOTV) drive must begin while other campaign activities are entering their most intensive stages, the GOTV coordinator must be someone who can act independently. This individual will be in charge of scheduling poll watchers, telephoners, drivers, babysitters, and a host of other workers. Fortunately, most of these positions can be filled by volunteers who have other assignments during the rest of the campaign.

The candidate is the most important person in the direct voter contact program. The field coordinator must ensure that the candidate's time scheduled for canvassing activities is put to optimal use. If he or she is good at one-to-one communication, and the campaign plan allows sufficient time, the candidate may be assigned the bulk of the initial voter contact work. But to be effective, the houses to be visited must be well-targeted, the candidate well-supported by aides and materials, and the follow-up must be systematic.

The Voter Contact Plan

To be successful, direct voter contact must be conducted systematically and repetitively. In smaller districts it may be possible to visit or call every home. But in larger districts there's not enough time, money, or volunteers to try to contact every potential voter. It doesn't make sense to spend time talking with people who are certain to vote for your opponent or unlikely to vote at all.

The targeting techniques discussed in Chapter 3 will help you identify those areas where your voter contact program will have the greatest effect. If the campaign only has resources to reach 50 percent of the district's households, priority should be given to the areas in the upper half of your targeting rankings.

Analyzing comparison races in the targeting process will also give you another important piece of information: an estimate of the number of votes you will need to win. This sets the campaign's goal and gives you a benchmark against which to measure your progress during the canvass.

Your written field organization plan should answer these questions:

- How many times will each prospective voter be contacted?

- When will voter contacts be made?

- What mix of door-to-door, telephone, mail, and group contacts will be used?

- Will the campaign try to register new voters? If so, how?

- How will you make sure supporters vote on Election Day?

The field operation must also have a timetable that sets deadlines for completion of a specified number of voter contacts. This is the only way all the work will be completed by Election Day. The best voter contact plans build momentum, starting slowly with voter identification work, following up with persuasion techniques for undecided voters and motivational activities aimed at supporters, and culminating with an all-out push to turn out likely voters.

Every campaign must keep detailed records to know what progress is being made in carrying out the plan. Data on every voter contact should be recorded and the results summarized. Periodically, the tallies should be analyzed to see if you are on schedule. Based on accurate feedback, strategy and timelines can be adjusted or resources redeployed to problem areas.

Identifying Voters

The first step in carrying out your voter contact plan is to develop a system to rate the attitudes of potential voters. The most simple scheme uses a 1-2-3 scale to identify voters:

- "1" = Favorable

- "2" = Undecided

- "3" = Unfavorable

If you have the capacity to make effective use of a more elabo-rate range of responses, we prefer a 1–5 system representing:

- "1" = Definite candidate support

- "2" = Leaning favorable

- "3" = Undecided

- "4" = Leaning unfavorable

- "5" = Definite opponent support

This is the identification system referred to throughout the rest of this chapter. Refining the distinctions further makes no sense. It simply creates additional burdens on the volunteers who are mak-ing the judgment, while not altering the campaign's post-canvass follow-up in any way.

It's also necessary to establish very clear guidelines for each category and to make sure everyone in the campaign uses the same standards. Have the strictest standards for identifying defi-nite supporters ("1s"). In some campaigns only those who have volunteered or made a contribution are rated "1." Decide how you will determine those who are favorable to the candidate ("2s"). Most likely, even if a voter is friendly to the canvasser and interested in receiving information, he or she should be rated as undecided ("3") unless specific statements favoring the candidate are made.

The Door-to-Door Canvass

In local races, the most productive technique for direct voter con-tact is the door-to-door canvass. Designed primarily to determine which voters should be treated as favorable, persuadable, or unfa-vorable, the canvass is simultaneously a way to deliver your mes-sage in person and recruit volunteers and donors. Campaigning door-to-door also allows you to solicit voters' support directly. House Speaker Thomas P. "Tip" O'Neill loves to tell the story of a lifelong family friend who didn't vote for him in a race he narrowly lost because, "You didn't ask for my vote."

By far the most persuasive contact can be made by the candidate. Personally asking for support is even more effective if it is in marked contrast to your opponent. When challenger John Houston met voters at the door, he introduced himself by saying he was running against a sixteen-year incumbent, implying, "When was the last time you saw Senator Foley?"

Although door-to-door canvassing yields the best results, geography and demographics may dictate other tactics in some districts. In rural communities, for example, distance between homes may rule out walking or even driving house-to-house. Though apartments may be close together in an urban complex, fear of crime may inhibit these prospective voters from opening the door to strangers. In these circumstances, the campaign may have to use telephone, mail, or group contact techniques.

But almost always, some part of the district can be canvassed on foot. *If your program is well targeted, going door-to-door is the surest way to win votes.*

Preparing Materials for the Canvass

Before canvassers can hit the streets, a tremendous amount of work must be done. Lists must be gathered, written materials prepared, and volunteers recruited and trained.

Lists of registered voters for target precincts or towns can usually be obtained from the local Elections Office. In some parts of the country it will be necessary to travel to the county seat or the state capital to get this information. Find out in advance if there is a fee involved or if it must be hand copied. Another alternative may be to rent copies of lists from commercial firms that have transcribed the names, addresses, and phone numbers of registered voters onto computer tapes.

Generally, you will want lists of only those people eligible to vote in the race in which you are running. In a closed primary this means only members of your own party. For a general election, you will want the full voters list.

If you have decided to target your campaign efforts to only those most likely to vote, you will also need to get the appropriate voting record histories to identify voters who cast ballots in at least two of the last three similar elections. Targeting individual, historic voters is tedious work, but the "cleaned" list will be a near perfect guide for focusing limited campaign resources.

All lists must be arranged to fit your canvassing needs. For a door-to-door canvass, the list must be put into walking order by streets. This often requires cutting apart or retyping material supplied by the election department into precinct or alphabetical order. Voters' names should be entered on a canvassing report form like the one on page 93 before canvassers set out.

In addition, a master file card like the sample below must be kept on each potential voter to record canvass data and monitor follow-up.

SAMPLE MASTER FILE CARD

Voter's Name _____
Support Rating _____
Address _____
Ward/Pct _____
Phone _____
Registered: Yes ☐ No ☐ Party Affiliation _____
Needs:
☐ More Info. _____   ☐ Volunteer
☐ Absentee Ballot   ☐ Canvass
☐ Drive to Polls   ☐ Election Day
☐ Election Day Child Care   ☐ Give Money
☐ Other _____
Additional Info. _____ _____
_____
_____

In most cases, it will also be necessary to add telephone numbers to facilitate phone calls to voters who were not home for the door-to-door canvass or to follow-up the initial contact. Looking up numbers is another time-consuming task. A reverse phone book, which lists subscribers by street address, is the easiest way to do this job. Try to borrow a copy from a library, real estate of-

CANVASSING REPORT FORM

(All items in the first three columns should be filled in before leaving HQ.)

Street Name _____ Community _____ Ward _____ Polling Place _____

House #	Voter's Name	Phone #	Rating	Comments	Follow-Up

Rating System: **1** = **Definite Support** **2** = **Favorable** **3** = **Undecided**
4 = **Unfavorable** **5** = **Supporting Opponent**
R = **Refused** **X** = **Not Home**

FOR HEADQUARTERS USE ONLY

☐ NOT AT HOMES RECONTACTED   ☐ FOLLOW-UP COMPLETED
☐ INFO. TRANSFERRED TO MASTER   ☐ DATA TABULATED

fice; or a local business. In any case, start adding phone numbers immediately so the process can be completed before the area is scheduled to be canvassed.

Don't count on previous campaigns to provide complete lists of current residents or voters. Because nearly a quarter of all Americans move each year, data from a previous contest will be substantially out-of-date. Information from past campaign's can be used to identify historic voters, but it's often easier to build your master list from scratch than to check hundreds or thousands of names and addresses for accuracy.

If your campaign has access to a personal computer, it can greatly simplify recordkeeping. Relatively simple data base management programs can be used to set up all the basic files you'll need. Volunteers can then enter names, addresses, and phone numbers as well as feedback from the canvass and other data. All this information can then be printed out in different formats for each of your campaign needs, including street walking lists and lists for telephone follow-up. The market is new, but there are a few commercial computer software programs designed especially for campaigns. These can cost from $500 to $1,500. You can do as well if you have the help of an experienced computer buff by adapting programs like dBase III by Ashton-Tate, or Lotus 1-2-3 to fit your needs. Be certain what information you need on each voter and what form you will need it in before you design your system.

In addition to lists, you must also prepare the materials needed to contact voters. Among the items required for street canvassing are literature to be left with the voters, postcards or letters for voters who are not home, and buttons, bumper stickers, and the like to give to supporters.

The two most important materials in the volunteers' kits are report forms and written instructions. The instructions should include a sample script like the one on page 95, which indicates the different responses for favorable, unfavorable, and undecided voters. Be sure all volunteers understand the system for recording voter identification information on the canvassing report form. Include a street map of the area to be covered and always list a phone number the volunteer can call if any problems arise.

Recruiting and Training Volunteers

As we said earlier, door-to-door canvassing by the candidate is by far the most persuasive voter contact technique. But even if your campaign plan calls for the candidate to canvass the high-priority areas, volunteers will still be needed for the lower priority areas,

★ **Susan Richards for Senator**

FOOT CANVASSER'S INSTRUCTION SHEET

Thank you for volunteering to help in our canvass. Your role is among the most important in the campaign. In a very real way, you are my personal representative in reaching voters.

The information you collect will help us make sure that we win every possible vote on Election Day.

I truly appreciate your support and hard work.

Susan Richards

SAMPLE SCRIPT

I.
"Good afternoon, I am _____ , a volunteer for Ms. Richards, who wants to represent you in the State Senate. Have you heard of Ms. Richards' campaign?

> **positive response:** "That's right. Ms. Richards is running because she believes people like us should receive better services from our state government." Go to Step II
>
> **negative response:** "Well, Ms. Richards is running to get better services for all of us. She thinks our town needs a new senior center, expanded day care, and an effective consumer protection agency." Go to Step II
>
> **hostile response:** "Thank you. I'm sorry to have bothered you." Go to next house on route.

II.
"Could I ask whether you plan to support Ms. Richards at the Primary Election on Tuesday, September 14?

> **yes:** "That's great. Will you need any assistance in getting to (polling place) to vote? Can you volunteer to help the campaign in any way? Would you like a bumpersticker, button, or lawn sign? Thank you very much." MARK RATING—1 or 2
>
> **maybe:** "Can I answer any questions that might help you decide? Would you like to examine Ms. Richards's literature? Thank you." MARK RATING—3
>
> **no or refuse to answer:** "Thank you. Good afternoon." MARK RATING—4 or Refused
>
> **supporting opponent:** "Thank you for taking the time to talk with me. Good-bye." MARK RATING—5

REMEMBER

- Avoid arguments. Keep conversations brief and friendly.
- Don't try to answer detailed questions about campaign positions if you are uncertain. Promise we'll call back. Make a note of the name, telephone number, and question and refer it to the canvass coordinator.
- Record all other information as soon as the discussion has ended.
- Leave literature under the door if no one is home. It is against the law to put it into the mailbox.
- If any problems arise, call 555-6543.
- Return to headquarters when you have completed your route and turn in all canvassing materials.

for follow-up houses missed by the candidate, or to contact voters in a second round of canvassing. Your canvassing program will therefore involve extensive recruiting and training of volunteers. The field director and volunteer coordinator should review the volunteer budget to determine how many canvassers will be required for all of your targeted areas.

Local field coordinators should play an important role in recruiting volunteers for the canvass in their area. The more personal the contact, the better. The endorsement of volunteers from their own neighborhood can be very persuasive for voters.

Consider how members of the candidate's family can assist with the canvass effort. It can be a plus for children to accompany the candidate, if they are old enough to be helpful rather than requiring attention themselves. The candidate's spouse, brothers or sisters, or even extended family members should be used if they are good spokespersons and enthusiastic supporters of the campaign. The most extensive family effort we've seen was Democrat John Houston's successful 1984 state senate race in Massachusetts. No fewer than fifty-four family members were active canvassing throughout the campaign. And, in this case, family loyalty clearly overrode partisan politics—many of the family members were Republican!

Optimally, canvassers should work in teams of two with one male and one female volunteer. Experience has shown that this arrangement is least threatening to voters and produces the fewest refusals to respond. Working together is also good for volunteer morale. But pairing up may strain the campaign's limited volunteer resources. As a compromise, try sending people into an area in teams, but assign only one individual to approach each home. Team members can work opposite sides of the street where they can keep each other in sight and talk if necessary.

The same approach should always be used with the candidate. It is most effective if he or she is totally free to talk with potential voters while the aide carries maps, street lists, and literature and records responses. The aide can also subtlely help the candidate avoid extended conversations.

At the beginning of each day's canvass, volunteers should be gathered together, given their canvassing kits, and fully briefed. This is a good time for an inspirational speech from the campaign manager or volunteer coordinator. A few words from the candidate at the beginning of the overall program will help convey the impression that canvassers are the personal representatives of your campaign. Take the time to touch on the objectives of the activity and major campaign issues. Canvassing is hard work. Make sure volunteers understand why their contribution is so important.

Carefully review the instruction sheet and all canvass materials. Individuals who have canvassed in other races may be familiar with different systems for recording voter preferences. Explain precisely what your codes mean and the specific standards for judging which category a voter falls into.

The training session should end with a role-playing exercise in which the volunteers confront typical situations. Divide the group into pairs and allow each person several opportunities to play canvasser and voter. The trainer should set up unusual, but not impossible, situations such as a parent opening the door carrying a crying baby or a slightly tipsy person who invites the canvasser in for a beer. Acting out these cases builds confidence, diffuses emotional tensions, and prepares volunteers for the unpredictable reactions they are likely to encounter.

A word of caution: candidates are notoriously bad at hearing unfavorable responses. Every campaign has its own version of this story told to us by the manager of a New Jersey campaign for state representative: reacting to a voter who slammed the door in his face and said, "Get out of here. You and your family are all crooks," the candidate turned to his aide and said, "Put her down as undecided." While volunteers' evaluations in your campaign will not, we hope, be this far out of line, you should caution your supporters to be conservative in their ratings. Especially as the campaign gains momentum, enthusiastic canvassers are likely to misrepresent the strength of a voter's support for the candidate. Stress that follow-up contacts and GOTV activities will only be effective if the initial ratings they record are accurate.

Recordkeeping and Follow-Up

Accurate records are necessary to ensure proper follow-up to the canvass, evaluate progress, and avoid overlap. An efficient system must be designed to transfer information from canvassing forms to more permanent records and to feed the names of appropriate supporters to other campaign components such as fundraising and volunteer recruitment.

At a minimum, favorable and unfavorable figures must be tallied and the results analyzed to detect trends. The total number of completed contacts should be checked regularly against canvassing benchmarks to determine if adjustments should be made in the voter contact plan. The data can also be used to evaluate the performance of individual volunteers. Here again, the use of computerized data processing will save considerable time.

Follow-up depends on the individual voter's response to the canvass. Requests for more information or specific questions must receive immediate attention. Potential volunteers or donors should be recontacted quickly to firm up their commitments. Names of voters needing transportation or child care on Election Day should be referred to the GOTV coordinator.

Your plan should include systematic follow-up to "leaning favorable" and "undecideds." It will take repeated, persuasive contacts to turn these into "1s," or definite votes, by Election Day. Depending on your resources, you can use a combination of the telephone, mail, and literature techniques described in the following sections.

Canvassing by Telephone

Some campaigns may choose to rely on the telephone to conduct the basic canvass. Though this mode of voter contact is less personal than campaigning door-to-door, basic information can still be obtained from prospective voters.

Phone canvassing may be mandated by geography or demographics, but in some situations it may also be the most efficient way to use scarce volunteer resources. Telephone callers can usually reach 50 percent more voters per hour than foot canvassers, and calls can be placed during evening hours by volunteers who hold daytime jobs. Depending on the number of volunteers at the campaign's disposal and the hours they are available, telephone canvassing may be the only way to get the work done.

Even if the telephone is not used for the initial canvass, it can be a valuable campaign tool for follow-up work. Phone calls are probably the best mechanism to contact individuals who were not at home during the door-to-door canvass. Calls may also be used to respond to voters' questions, thank supporters, draw in potential volunteers, or invite undecided voters to candidate coffees or other events. Telephone calls are quite appropriate for the second round of direct contacts in campaigns that want to reinforce the positions of favorable voters.

Whatever purpose it is designed to serve, a telephone canvass is set up in much the same way as the foot canvass. Accurate lists must be acquired and phone numbers added. Canvassers have to be recruited, trained, and monitored. Unlike volunteers who go door-to-door, the appearance of phone canvassers is not important. But voice quality, including speaking pace and accents, and telephone manners are.

The volunteer kits for telephone canvassers should always contain a prepared script such as the sample below. Be sure volunteers understand the responses and how to record them for each voter called.

As always, records must be carefully maintained and evaluated. Don't fall behind in transferring the results of each day's phoning into your master files. It's the only way necessary follow-up will be completed in a timely manner.

Telephoning from a central phone bank is preferable to having volunteers call from home. Though home-based phone calls may avoid toll charges for message units, there's less opportunity for

SAMPLE TELEPHONE CANVASSING SCRIPT

STEP I. "Good afternoon, I am (your name) , a volunteer for Howard Donnelly who wants to represent you in the State Senate. Have you heard of Mr. Donnelly's campaign?"

POSITIVE RESPONSE: "That's right. Mr. Donnelly is running because he believes people like us should receive better services from state government."

GO TO STEP II.

NEGATIVE RESPONSE: "Well, Mr. Donnelly is running to get better services for all of us. He thinks our town needs a new senior citizens' center, expanded day care, and an effective consumer protection agency."

GO TO STEP II.

HOSTILE RESPONSE: "Thank you. I'm sorry to have bothered you."

HANG UP. RATE AS 4. CALL NEXT NUMBER ON LIST.

STEP II. "Could I ask whether you plan to vote for Mr. Donnelly at the primary election on Tuesday, September 14?"

YES: "That's great. Will you need assistance in getting to (local polling place) to vote? Can you help the campaign by becoming a volunteer? Can I send you a bumpersticker or lawn sign? Thank you very much."

RATE AS 1 or 2.

NO OR REFUSE TO ANSWER: "Thank you."

RATE AS 4 or R.

MAYBE: "Can I answer any questions that might help you decide? I will send you further information about Mr. Donnelly's campaign. Thank you."

RATE AS 3.

monitoring and supervision. The biggest risk is having volunteers take a list home and not complete the calls.

Phone banks can be run from campaign headquarters if you have an adequate number of lines. But installation can become a very expensive proposition since local phone companies extract large deposits from political campaigns. Your best bet may be a friendly business, labor union, or civic organization that has multiple phone lines. Be careful to check your state's campaign finance laws to determine whether the use of telephones is considered an in-kind contribution. You may have to sign a rental agreement and pay for all message units and long distance charges to avoid the appearance of an illegal contribution from a corporation or union.

If you allow reliable volunteers to phone canvass from home, evaluate their performance regularly by examining feedback sheets and making occasional check-up calls by randomly selecting names on their lists. Only give a volunteer twenty or thirty names at a time. A huge list can make working from home an intimidating prospect. It's better to assign just enough names for one or two night's work. A smaller number gives volunteers a sense of accomplishment; at the same time, the campaign doesn't run the risk of hundreds of prospective voters not being called.

For all telephone work, certain basic rules prevail. Most important of all, make sure telephoners understand your campaign's rating system to identify voters. Don't waste time calling when people are likely to be away from home, busy preparing meals or eating, or sleeping. The most productive times for calls are from 7:00 to 9:00 every evening and on weekend afternoons. In rural districts where sunrise chores are common, calling should end even earlier.

Print Communication with Voters

Every campaign uses some form of printed literature to help get its message across to voters. The actual designing and producing of these materials is discussed in Chapter 7; what we will cover here is how they can be used as a part of your voter contact program.

Both direct mail and leaflets can be used as a follow-up to reinforce other more personal techniques or to make your initial contact with voters. In the latter case, they are often used to increase name recognition in advance of a canvass. The timing and the sequence will depend on your campaign plan.

The major limitation of these vehicles is that they usually only provide for one-way communication. Unlike the canvass, you cannot assess the voter's reaction. Even when postpaid mail-back forms are designed into the printed material, it's much less likely that a voter will respond to a mailing than a phone call or visit.

Campaign Leaflets

Literature "drops" are a fast and inexpensive way to distribute campaign information to potential voters. Volunteers leave the leaflet at each home, but make no effort to talk with voters. Targeting can be done either by geographic area or by using voter registration or historic voter lists to identify individual households. If you have enough volunteers you can deliver leaflets without incurring the costs of the U.S. Postal Service.

Like canvassers, leafleteers need preparation in order to do their job effectively. Prepare written instructions and answer any questions before volunteers set out. Maps are mandatory as are street lists if the drop is to be targeted. Remember, it is a violation of federal law to put leaflets into home mailboxes. Leave them inside the screen door, or roll them up and attach them to the doorknob with a rubber band.

Direct Mail

Direct mail is a more effective way to communicate with voters in writing, but it is also more expensive. The main advantage is that you can tailor your communication to the specific audience you are trying to reach. By using different letters with different segments of your lists you can reach members of a specialized constituency in a manner that addresses their particular concerns. Lists may be segmented by geographic area and stress local neighborhood concerns, such as highway construction, proposed development, or school problems. Or specific constituencies can be mailed to from district-wide lists. For example, one successful Wisconsin candidate supporting no-fault automobile insurance cross-matched voter registration and vehicle registration lists to target an audience he felt would be receptive to his campaign. Just prior to the election, voters received a skillfully produced letter two to three days after volunteers "dropped" a campaign leaflet that contained reprints of a newspaper article on rising insurance rates. These persuasive communications reinforced the candidate's appearances and a five-week-long canvass effort by volunteers.

Voter Contact Through Groups

Your campaign can contact voters in three types of groups. Frequently its focus will be a broad range of formal organizations, such as civic clubs, business associations, and neighborhood organizations. These may also include special constituencies such as women's, minority, and senior citizens' organizations or issue groups. You may also want to relate to informal collections of non-affiliated individuals who simultaneously gather in groups at supermarkets, mass transit stops, or special events. Finally, most campaigns organize their own groups for specific purposes, like candidate coffees.

Direct candidate contact with all three types of groups is covered in Chapter 4. But even if the candidate is unable to appear in person, the campaign should schedule voter contact programs for organizations that are important in the campaign plan. A family member or campaign representative may speak on behalf of the candidate. Volunteers may pass out campaign literature or set up an information table.

Formal endorsements should be sought from organized groups. Those statements of support (which amount to the "Good Housekeeping Seal of Approval") can be publicized by the press secretary. But endorsements are even more valuable to motivate individuals who are members of the organization. Ask each group to back up their endorsement with concrete support. Depending on the capacity and effectiveness of the organization, internal tasks can include distributing campaign materials to members, publicity about the candidate in the newsletter or bulletin, and conducting voter registration and GOTV drives among members.

To the extent possible, coordinate the groups' activities with the campaign's voter contact plan. Follow up and monitor the group's progress. Don't assume the work is being done. In addition, associations that support your candidate should also be asked to recruit volunteers to staff major campaign activities such as canvassing drives and Election Day.

The crowds that gather for special events such as parades, sports contests, and concerts give the campaign an opportunity to reach very large numbers of people. Access is limited only by your imagination and local laws governing campaigning on private property. Leafleting events is an easy way to increase the campaign's visibility. Know the likely make-up of the crowd before you invest more than token resources. Consider how many of the people who take your literature will live outside the district or not be registered to vote.

Get Out The Vote (GOTV)

Despite months of hard work, campaigns are won or lost in one day. Election Day is the culmination of your entire effort. Every available resource should be devoted to turning out the candidate's supporters to vote. And as many a candidate who has won or lost by a razor thin margin will tell you, every vote counts.

The well-planned campaign will have carefully identified its supporters through the canvass and systematically followed up to keep favorable voters in the fold. Your repeated contacts with favorables and undecideds will, we hope, have persuaded a sufficient number to support your candidate. Now the task is to translate support into votes by getting your favorable voters to the polls.

The first decisions involve which voters to turn out. Your "1s" are definite votes and all GOTV plans should emphasize these voters. Your strategy for dealing with "2s" and "3s" will depend on your campaign plan and how the numbers have developed throughout the canvass and voter persuasion efforts. If a voter was initially identified as favorable and has received subsequent persuasion contacts by the campaign, that person is probably a likely enough support vote to be "pulled" on Election Day. If your canvass numbers project that you will have a winning vote count simply by adding your "1s" and "2s," limit your GOTV efforts to these voters.

If that is not the case, as is most often true, you have to make a judgment call about those you have rated as "3" or undecided. One piece of information to consider are reliable polls (whether your own, your party's, or the local newspaper). They can help you estimate what percentage of the undecided vote will break for you. Unless you feel sure that a majority of undecideds will vote for your candidate, don't focus any GOTV efforts on them. Otherwise you'll be helping your opponent. Another option is to pull undecided voters in only those areas where there has been extensive campaign activity or where the canvass numbers show strong support for your candidate. In those areas, the campaign's momentum can be expected to push a higher percentage of undecided voters into your camp.

The GOTV pull can begin several days in advance with phone calls and postcards reminding supporters of voting locations and the hours polls are open—these reminders can be signed by the candidate—or campaign volunteers can be asked to mail "Dear Friend" cards to their neighbors. These can be printed like the sample below, or even better, have the cards individually handwritten. These can be prepared well in advance.

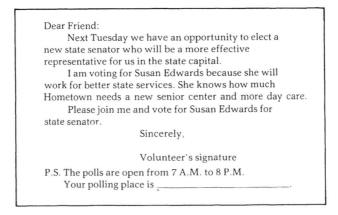

Dear Friend:
     Next Tuesday we have an opportunity to elect a new state senator who will be a more effective representative for us in the state capital.
     I am voting for Susan Edwards because she will work for better state services. She knows how much Hometown needs a new senior center and more day care.
     Please join me and vote for Susan Edwards for state senator.
          Sincerely,

          Volunteer's signature
P.S. The polls are open from 7 A.M. to 8 P.M.
     Your polling place is _____.

In some communities "door hangers," or literature with a "Don't forget to vote for (candidate)" message, are commonly used. Volunteers usually deliver these to supporters' home the night before the election.

On Election Day you should schedule several rounds of reminders to make sure all identified supporters vote. If it is legal in your jurisdiction, assign volunteers to be poll watchers to check off the names of your identified voters, or "1s" and "2s," as they enter each polling place. This information must be periodically reported to your Election Day headquarters or to the local GOTV coordinator for each area. "Runners" can be used for this purpose, or poll watchers can relay the lists when their shifts end. Volunteers can then contact those supporters who have not yet voted and encourage or assist them to get to the polls. If you are unable to use poll watchers, you will have to contact all the voters you have decided to pull.

GOTV contacts usually start about 1:00 P.M. after some voters have had a chance to get to the polls. At this time start your afternoon contacts with senior citizens and others who you expect to be home during the day. Depending on your resources, a variety of pulling techniques can be used. Telephone calls are the easiest. You will need a phone bank or multiple phones in supporters' homes in order to complete all the contacts. This operation can be decentralized by town or precinct, but good supervision is essential. With enough volunteers, it is possible to go door-to-door in key neighborhoods and ring the doorbells of supporters who have not voted. Leave reminder notes on the doors of families who are not home.

The pulling effort becomes more intense after 5:00 P.M., since many working people will not have voted yet. It is important to get supporters to the polls before they settle in for an evening at home. Encourage everyone you talk with to vote before sitting down to dinner.

An hour before the polls close, you should launch one last blitz of phone calls or home visits. Emphasize that their vote can be the margin of victory in that precinct. Volunteers should be willing to do anything from babysitting to stirring the dinner stew if that is what it takes to get a favorable voter to the polls. Don't worry about using high pressure techniques at this stage. The worst that can happen is that the person will still refuse to vote. It's very unlikely that you will cause a supporter to change his or her mind and cast a ballot for your opponent.

The highest priority Election Day tasks described above are designed to get out your vote. Once these positions are filled, additional volunteers can be assigned to holding signs and/or handing out literature at polling sites. These visibility efforts can be helpful if your race is way down the ballot. Some undecided voters may well make up their mind about the lesser offices at the last minute.

Actually, surveys have shown that this technique can add several percentage points to a candidate's vote total, but only in cases where the electorate is largely ignorant of the race. If an aggressive voter contact campaign has already been waged, leafleteers at the polls on Election Day will have very little impact. The only message you can deliver at this point is a reminder of the candidate's name and the office. Keep any signs or leaflets simple.

Especially if your GOTV efforts are decentralized with follow-up calls being made from several locations, be sure all coordinators can communicate quickly and easily with headquarters. Always reserve some telephone lines to be kept open for incoming calls.

If possible, your Get Out the Vote drive should not be conducted in a vacuum. Talk with other campaigns who are planning similar efforts. Cooperative arrangements can be made with friendly candidates to share resources such as reports from poll watchers. Organizations that support the candidate can also be asked to run GOTV campaigns within their own members. There's nothing wrong if a potential voter is contacted by two or three different sources on Election Day. As long as they support the candidate, the only important thing is that they get to the polls and vote. That is what your whole campaign has been all about.

Absentee Voting

Before you quickly bypass this section let us assure you that absentee ballots have been the deciding factor in many state and local campaigns, including the extremely close race for the governor of California in 1984. The outcome of a very tight contest can be reversed once these ballots are counted. Depending on your constituency, it may make sense to incorporate a program for absentee voting into your campaign plan.

First, carefully review local laws to determine the method of applying for an absentee ballot as well as the methods for certifying and mailing. If your state allows campaign workers to be deputized to handle absentee ballots, have the volunteers assigned to this program deputized.

Like all other parts of the voter contact program, the absentee ballot program should be targeted to your likely supporters. This usually done in two ways. The first is to visit senior citizens' homes and other institutions where potential voters may find it difficult to get to the polls on Election Day. Always make advance arrangements with the administration to determine the best times to contact voters.

The second method involves responding to requests for absentee ballots that are generated by the campaign's door-to-door or telephone canvass. All campaign workers should be briefed on the proper procedures and refer supporters' requests to the field director. Set up a system to ensure that all requests are handled promptly.

Voter Registration

In most parts of the country, people who are not properly registered cannot vote, no matter how strongly they feel about your candidate. Your campaign shouldn't count on these individuals unless you have ample time, money, and volunteers to launch a voter registration drive and a GOTV plan to get them to the polls. This is seldom true of individual state and local campaigns.

Except in isolated cases, such as the first-time candidacy of a minority group leader, registration drives seldom have a major impact on the composition of the electorate. Your campaign strategy must be based on the fact that the most likely voters in your election will be those who have consistently voted in the past, and that is where most of the campaign's resources should be concentrated.

In the event your campaign planning concludes that new registrants can provide the margin needed for victory, look first to your political party or other organizations in your community that may already be preparing a voter registration project. The candidate may even be able to encourage state or local public officials to conduct the drive. Beginning in 1984, several states, including Ohio and New Mexico, set up facilities to register new voters at all government offices, including the unemployment compensation and public welfare departments. If others take the basic responsibility, your campaign can then supplement these registration drives. All the campaign's efforts should be targeted to its own priority constituencies and to those areas most likely to produce the highest percentage of favorable voters for your candidate. All this may not sound like textbook civics, but a campaign manager who sets up a program that registers mainly the opponent's voters is in the wrong job.

The most effective registration drives are run like voter identification canvasses. Cross-check reverse phone books or census data with current voter registration records to identify unregistered voters in your target areas. Compile lists with names and addresses. Put these in volunteer canvass kits along with the necessary street maps and reporting forms. Laws governing residency requirements, deadlines, and filing procedures must be carefully researched. Then conduct a training seminar for volunteers in which you give detailed instructions on how to get the people they contact onto the voting rolls.

In some jurisdictions, volunteers can be appointed special registrars who can enroll people at their homes or in public places. If this method is legal in your district, campaign volunteers can set up registration tables at locations where likely supporters congregate. Check the regulations concerning passing out campaign literature at the same time.

Even with a systematic effort, voter registration is hard work. While a well-organized drive can have positive results over a long period of time, progress is often much slower than the fast-approaching deadlines of a campaign. And to be effective, it takes a second effort to turn out new registrants to vote. If you decide to undertake a registration project you should be sure it will pay off with more votes on Election Day than you'd get if you devoted the same money and volunteers to other campaign work.

6

FREE MEDIA

In this electronic age, national campaigns have become media marathons. Presidential candidates and their running mates spend most of their waking moments in airplanes, touching down only briefly to make cameo appearances in as many as five different media markets each day. Only the tiniest percentage of the electorate has any personal contact with the candidate. The rest rely on "mediated" communications delivered by TV, radio, and local newspapers.

It should seem obvious that this heavy reliance on media, while crucial for national or statewide elections, is a poor model for local campaigns. Yet, all too often, municipal and legislative candidates overestimate the role of the media. As a result, they frequently spend too much time trying to talk to reporters instead of talking to voters.

Put simply, media cannot carry a local campaign by itself. We know of countless incumbents lulled into complacency by extensive media coverage who were defeated by challengers who gathered votes one-by-one campaigning door-to-door.

To be effective, media must be balanced with the other components of your campaign. News coverage and advertising are most productively used to reinforce personal messages delivered through repetitive direct contacts made by the candidate and your field organization. Media efforts, in concert with other campaign activities, can help build momentum. Meeting the candidate in person, then hearing an excerpt from a campaign speech on the radio, and finally receiving a leaflet or letter on the same theme creates the repetition needed for victory.

The advantage of media communications is that you can reach large numbers of people simultaneously. Using the media effectively can thus increase your capacity to contact and persuade target voters. Even before your campaign is formally launched, media can play an important role in establishing your public identity. Name recognition from positive coverage of your civic, business, or charitable activities will give your campaign an initial boost. Certainly, no one can support you unless they first know your name. Early media coverage may also create credibility with potential donors and endorsers. And it provides valuable feedback to workers who need to know their efforts are making an impact.

In political campaigns there are two types of indirect or "mediated" communications: free media, often called news coverage; and paid media, or advertising. Free media includes newspaper, radio or television stories, and candidate exposure through organizational newsletters, bulletins, and other periodicals. Paid media refers to electronic spots and print ads for which the campaign must buy time or space as well as literature and such campaign paraphernalia as buttons and bumper stickers.

We'll look at free media first because, unlike advertising, which requires significant expenses for production and placement, press and publicity work can reach large audiences at minimal cost. In a low budget campaign, coverage in the news may be the only practical way to deliver your message simultaneously to target voters. Paid media is covered in the following chapter.

The Press Secretary

Dealing with the press is one of your campaign's toughest jobs. Many different activities must be coordinated on very tight deadlines. Generally, supervision of all facets of media relations is assigned to a single staff person who is most often given the title of press secretary.

Someone who knows the ropes and has established personal relationships with some members of the local press is likely to be the best person to handle this important responsibility. Consider press aides from previous campaigns or media coordinators from citizens' groups in your area. Journalism faculty and recent graduates from college public relations programs also have great potential for this role.

The press secretary must be a person with multiple skills. Most important are the abilities to recognize news, write effective releases quickly, and convince reporters that stories are worth covering. Whoever is chosen must be a person the candidate trusts completely since the press secretary will play an important role in establishing the campaign's public image and credibility.

Execution of the media plan allows many roles for volunteers working under the direction of the press secretary. List maintenance, monitoring coverage, telephoning, and typing can all be done at home or at headquarters by volunteers, but to avoid errors and confusion, the campaign cannot have a host of spokespeople. The press secretary should be the only person besides the candidate, and possibly the campaign manager, who talks with reporters and editors. If volunteers are assigned any direct media contact work, they should be thoroughly briefed and provided with written scripts for making phone calls.

For everyone working with the media, there are basic rules of behavior. Reporters will be more inclined to give favorable coverage to campaigns that treat them as professionals and help them do their difficult jobs more effectively. Here are some of the most important guidelines:

• The cardinal rule is *always tell the truth*. If you don't know the facts, admit it. Promise to check details and get back quickly with accurate information.

• *Keep the candidate informed*. Never put out a press release that the candidate has not seen and approved. The candidate should never be caught off guard by a reporter's question about a campaign story he or she is not familiar with.

• *Remain accessible at all times*. Return phone calls promptly so reporters can meet deadlines. Be polite when contacted at home, late at night, on holidays, or weekends.

• *Know the rules*. Recognize that all conversations with reporters and editors are "on the record" with both your name and every word you say subject to publication unless you and the journalist agree otherwise before you begin talking. "Not for attribution" is for occasions when you don't want your name in the paper but don't mind the use of an anonymous quote from "a campaign official." "Background" means the information may be used, but not quoted or attributed to any source. Finally, "off the record" means the information may not be printed or broadcast in any manner.

● *Be aggressive.* A late story is no story at all. Call in breaking news and reactions. Volunteer story ideas, but don't demand coverage.

● *Be fair.* Always treat competing members of the media equally. If you play favorites the other reporters are likely to disregard your routine releases. If you do exclusive interviews, spread them around during the course of the campaign.

● *Never exaggerate.* If you get the reputation for inflating stories or overpromising the size of events, the media will view the campaign's future claims with cynicism.

● *Don't use high pressure tactics.* Never use pressure or influence to try to get coverage. It's not likely to work, and throwing your weight around is certain to make enemies among the working press, which will harm the campaign in the long run.

● *Don't just criticize.* Point out errors when they occur, but also praise an accurate story or thoughtful analysis.

● *Try to keep the media from intimidating you.* Reporters' agendas are not the same as your campaign's. A balance must be struck between the media's needs and the campaign's strategy. Don't get diverted from your campaign plan by allowing a journalist to define the issues.

● And, finally, *don't ever give up.* Even the slickest public relations professionals send out many releases that end up in the wastebasket. Constantly evaluate to improve your performance, but never stop trying to get more free coverage.

The Free Media Plan

Media work cannot be conducted in isolation. To be effective, it must be coordinated with the other parts of your campaign. Contrary to popular belief, all press is not good press. Candidates for public office should ignore the adage, "I don't care what they say about me so long as they spell my name right." Coverage only helps if it's positive and if target audience, delivery mechanisms, and timing all mesh with your overall plan.

The fact that press work is relatively inexpensive should not be an excuse for treating free media with less discipline than any other facet of the campaign. As a key part of your communication strategy, it deserves careful planning.

During the course of the campaign, your media goals may change. The initial weeks may be devoted to building name recognition. Subsequent time may focus on fleshing-out public perceptions of the candidate through news stories that complement the final weeks of your canvassing efforts.

The goal of media coverage, as with all voter contact activities, is to "peak" just before Election Day. Time your media work to build for maximum exposure in the final period when voters are making up their minds.

At all stages, the campaign must have a free media plan framed by answering these basic questions:

- What communications channels reach target audiences in your district?

- What tools can be used to deliver your message?

- Which outlets will you pursue for coverage?

- What are the legal limitations on your ability to compel the media to tell your story?

To begin developing a free media plan, look first at the master campaign calendar. That timetable will identify scores of events that provide opportunities for coverage from the kick-off announcement right through fundraising events, candidate debates, and endorsements up to the Election Night victory statement.

A good rule of thumb is to have at least one event each week that merits coverage in the local media. That way you will be sure that weekly papers in the district always have access to a story about your candidate. There's no upper limit to how much press coverage you should seek. This is a case where the press secretary's experience, news sense, and knowledge of the district is crucial in determining when a good media campaign becomes counterproductive overkill. Just remember to concentrate your strongest stories in the days immediately before the election.

Think creatively about how to fill gaps in the initial schedule. At times you'll want to suggest activities to the campaign manager simply to have something for the media to cover. However, make sure these "media events" are designed to deliver your basic message. Press coverage is important, but it should play a reinforcing role and not be the driving force in your campaign.

Outlet Survey

Before you can select the best communications channels to reach your target audiences, you must first conduct a media survey in which you list every communications outlet in your district, determine the audience it reaches, and identify key personnel and requirements for access.

Getting accurate information is time consuming, but not difficult. Lists of electronic media serving your area may even appear in the telephone Yellow Pages or in the TV/Radio section of your local newspaper. More details are included in the volumes of *Broadcasting Yearbook* and *Standard Rate and Data* found in many libraries. For print outlets consult *Editor & Publisher's Yearbook* or *Ayer's Directory of Newspapers and Periodicals.* Local press associations and clipping services that monitor news coverage may also publish media directories.

Don't forget such wire services as Associated Press and United Press International, which may have electronic and print subscribers in your district. Also include "daybooks," commercial ventures that provide lists of the coming days' activities to many outlets.

Never assume that the standard guides include all possible outlets for campaign news and advertising. Make a special effort to dig up names of specialized communications vehicles that reach your target audience. These may include college papers and radio stations, minority community publications, organization newsletters, special interest periodicals, and club bulletins. If you are trying to reach voters over age sixty-five, for example, search out newsletters from senior citizens' groups and retired workers associations.

Once every outlet has been located, the next step is determining the audience each reaches. This information is usually available directly from the business department of each outlet since they rely on the data to sell advertising. Newspaper rate cards and electronic media survey books put out by rating services such as Arbitron and Nielsen also present many of the relevant figures.

Pay special attention to studies that break down the outlet's audiences according to time in the programming day or newspaper section. This information will be especially useful in directing you to individual shows or writers most likely to reach your target audience. The sports pages, for example, have a higher readership among men than women. A midday talk show, on the other hand, will have a predominantly female audience. You may be able to reach large numbers of senior citizens directly through a Golden Age column or show. Don't assume that conventional stereotypes are automatically accurate, however. Always check to make sure your biases are justified by the facts.

It is also necessary to determine what forms of coverage and advertising are possible at each station or publication:

- Is a certain amount of time or space allotted to each candidate before Election Day?

- What are the limits and deadlines for purchasing ads?

- Does the outlet produce editorials endorsing candidates?

- How are feature stories developed or assigned?

- Are there special mechanical requirements for material they will use?

The answers to all these questions should be carefully recorded in the campaign's media directory. Use a looseleaf notebook with one sheet per outlet. This will allow sufficient space for collecting all the information you will need. And you can use the reverse side as a log to record your contacts with the outlet and the resulting coverage of your campaign. Adapt the sample media survey form found on pages 117 and 118 for your own use. For every listing you'll need:

- The outlet's name, mailing address, and phone number

- The titles and names of key reporters, editors, and sales people

- Numbers on audience size and demographics

- Technical data such as deadlines and photo requirements

- Special policies toward candidates such as not covering campaign news conferences.

116

CAMPAIGN MEDIA SURVEY

Outlet Name _____ Type _____

Mailing Address _____ Phone _____

Street Address/Hand Delivery Directions _____

_____

Circulation/Rating _____ Major Audience _____

Deadlines: News _____ Photos _____

Advertising _____ Announcements _____

Key Personnel:

Title	Name	Office Phone	Home Phone
Owner/Publisher			
News Editor			
Editorial Writer			
Political Reporters			
Ad. Sales Director			

Planned Campaign Coverage _____

_____

_____

Special Requirements _____

_____

_____

Advertising Rates (Attach Rate Card if Available) _____

_____

Date info. entered/updated _____

(over for record of contact/coverage)

Make sure all data is precise and spelled correctly. Though previous campaigns in the same district may have gathered similar information, media personnel and policies change rapidly. Always check every entry to make sure it is up to date.

SAMPLE MEDIA CONTACT & COVERAGE LOG

Date	Nature of Contact	Outcome/Coverage	Follow-Up	Initial
(e.g. 8/2)	Mailed announcement release to managing editor	Nothing printed	Call to inquire	*JB.*
8/5	Called managing editor	Told release should go to political reporter	Change list	*RT.*

Attach additional sheets if necessary

Be certain you have identified all the major communications channels in your district by asking people in the target audiences what they read, watch, and hear. A comprehensive media survey that gets information from both outlets and target audiences ensures that no important delivery mechanism is overlooked.

Tools of the Trade

If you have a media plan designed to reinforce your overall campaign strategy, implementation becomes largely mechanical. Success will depend on how skillfully you use the tools of the trade to get your message across. "Newsworthiness" is vital, but the definition is subjective. Most reporters and editors will opt for a well-presented story that is easy to cover rather than a more complex issue that requires considerable time to dig out.

Skillful use of the "tools of the trade" will pay off in increased coverage. Most important are:

- Lists

- News releases

- Press kits

- Photos

- Actualities

- Media events

- News conferences

Let's examine each tool.

Lists

A campaign strategy based on heavy use of free media can only be as good as the quality of the names, addresses, and phone numbers in your media directory. If you have a newsworthy message but don't send it to the right people, you will lose valuable opportunities for free coverage. The information generated as part of your outlet survey must be translated into lists that can be used for quick and efficient delivery of campaign materials.

List styles will vary depending upon your planned application. For mailing news releases, the names, outlets, and addresses of reporters and editors should be typed in label format. Include titles when possible in case the individual on your list has gone on vacation or changed jobs. This guarantees that the person currently fill-ing the position will receive the mailing. If you plan to call in sto-ries to radio stations, you'll need a list of news editors along with a newsroom phone number that is hooked up to a tape recorder.

A good way to maintain addresses is to use pressure-sensitive labels that can be photocopied to create multiple sets. Typing on gummed labels interleaved with carbon paper produces an accept-able if slightly messier substitute. Both types are found in office supply stores. It is even possible to have volunteers hand address envelopes, but this needless repetition can be too time consuming. Of course, if your campaign has access to a computer, media lists can be filed and run off on labels, as you need them.

No matter what system you choose, keep several extra sets of stamped, preaddressed envelopes and up-to-date phone lists on hand at all times. Nothing is worse than delaying an important re-lease or phone story because the copier or computer holding the master list is "down" or labels are not typed.

It is also useful to set up a list of key outlets arranged according to walking or driving routes for times when information will be hand-delivered rather than mailed. One technique is to paste each label on an index card and then add travel directions from the pre-vious outlet on the route. Number the cards so the order can be maintained. Although such lists are particularly useful for emer-gencies, in-person delivery is always helpful since it presents an opportunity to sell your story and explain the information. The same person should be responsible for all deliveries so that per-sonal relationships can be developed with reporters and editors.

For responding to inquiries or following up mail contacts, a list of office and home phone numbers of editors and reporters at key outlets is required. Keep a copy in the campaign headquarters at all times and make sure another copy travels with your candidate.

You should also maintain certain specialized media lists. The names, addresses, and phone numbers of talk show producers may be important if you plan to seek exposure on these programs. So is similar information about editorial board members, colum-nists, and feature writers. Pay special attention to the men and women responsible for community calendars and other services that may publicize the time and place of upcoming events. These people may not be sent every media mailing from your campaign, but you must have quick access to their names, addresses, and phone numbers for the occasions when you need them.

For some applications, the master media list will have to be subdivided by type of outlet, deadlines, and appropriate content. Campus media, weeklies, and organization newsletters are among those that may occasionally require special treatment.

Keeping a large variety of media lists up to date may seem time consuming, but the extra work will result in fewer missed opportunities for coverage.

News Releases

The written news release is the standard device for conveying campaign information to the media. A release can serve a variety of purposes, including telling a story (before or after the event), issuing a statement, announcing an upcoming event, or filling in background facts.

Your overall campaign strategy will determine when releases should be sent out. Remember that the coverage generated by news releases must reinforce your other campaign activities. Decisions about the desired level of early media visibility are particularly complex. Some coverage may be necessary to build credibility and assist fundraising and volunteer recruiting efforts. However, if you're a challenger whom the "political pros" don't take seriously, you may not want early media coverage that spurs the incumbent into campaigning actively.

If you decide that releases are in order, your campaign timetable will offer dozens of opportunities, starting with the candidate's announcement. After that, you may decide the opening of campaign headquarters or the hiring of top staff merit publicity. Other appropriate topics include:

- Policy statements by the candidate

- Endorsements by prominent individuals or organizations (see sample on page 126)

- Appointment of local community coordinators

- Announcement of major campaign events

Releases may also focus on topics geared for coverage from a human interest angle, such as a story about the candidate's family or an unusual volunteer. Always remember to work your campaign theme into the story. The final news release will usually feature the candidate's victory or concession statement.

Even though you have set up comprehensive lists, don't get caught in the trap of sending out nothing but "all-purpose" releases. It is often worth the time to write a story that may be appropriate for only a handful of outlets or even just one newspaper. Tailoring some of your releases to the needs of different outlets is a sure way to increase coverage. For example, if several small newspapers serve different communities in your district, write a separate release for each one with a story about the appointment of your local town coordinator. A sample of a localized release appears on page 123.

Since they are used so frequently, good news releases are the cornerstone of effective media work. The best way to get your stories into print or onto the airwaves is to design releases that meet the needs of the target media. Too many releases end up in the wastebasket because they arrive late or are poorly written or sloppily produced.

Editors must scan dozens of releases every day. Since there is rarely time to read beyond the first couple of paragraphs, the story has to catch the reader's attention immediately. Always follow the "law of diminishing importance" in drafting your releases. Use a short, snappy headline that includes the most interesting "newspeg." Answer the basic journalistic questions Who, What, When, Where, Why, and How in the first one or two sentences. Include a pithy quote from the candidate as soon as possible.

Use the remaining paragraphs to fill out details and provide background, but don't expect information toward the end of the release to appear in most coverage. Editors are accustomed to releases written in "inverted pyramid" style with the most important news at the top. If there is too little space or time to run the entire story, they will often cut from the bottom up.

There are also certain conventions that should always be followed. Write short declarative sentences in the third person. Use action verbs whenever possible. Stick to the facts; value judgments, allegations, and conclusions should be confined to direct quotations. Always focus on specifics rather than generalities. Know the source for every fact and check all figures and spellings.

Reread the draft several times to make certain it conveys key points effectively. Eliminate confusing phrases, spell out potentially confusing abbreviations and explain complex points. Then, check the entire release to make sure it consistently delivers the campaign's message to your target audience.

Produce the release in a professional manner. Use the campaign's letterhead if any has been printed. Or have a volunteer with graphics skills design a simple, attractive form that can be

---

★ **Diane Walters for Senator**

For Information Contact:

Spokesperson ### - ####

(home) ### - ####

For Immediate Release

_____ NAMED LOCAL WALTERS FOR SENATE HEAD

(Name) of (Street Address) has been named the Hometown coordinator of Diane Walters's State Senate campaign. (Name) who has been active in the (local name) organization will be responsible for organizing events and a door-to-door canvass to help Ms. Walters reach local voters.

Ms. Walters explained the appointment, "We are delighted that (name) has taken the important job of organizing our campaign in Hometown. (His/Her) experience with community groups will help us deliver our message of a more responsive state government to local voters."

(Name) added, "I took on this volunteer assignment because I think all of us will be better off with Diane Walters in the State Senate. But I can't do the entire job myself. Anyone else who wants to volunteer should call me at home at (number) or leave a message for me at Walters campaign headquarters at 555-5678."

— 30 —

Note to editors: A photograph of (coordinator's name) with State Senate candidate Diane Walters is attached.

---

used for all releases. This can be done cheaply with rub-off letters available from art or office supply stores. Try using colored paper to make the release stand out.

At the top, include a date indicating when the release may be used. If it is designed for publication or broadcast as soon as it is received by the outlet, use "For Immediate Release." If not, indicate a date, for example: "For Release on May 20."

Just below the release date, type the name of the press secretary and both daytime and evening phone numbers. This is for use by reporters or editors who need to reach a campaign spokesperson to clarify the story.

Every release should have a headline that summarizes its major message. Type the headline in all capital letters and center it above the first line of the text to make it stand out.

Type the body of the release double-spaced with margins of at least an inch and a half on all sides to allow for editing. If more than one page is required, write "more" at the bottom of the first sheet and place a brief phrase identifying the story (e.g., "Campaign Kick-Off") and the number "2" at the top of the second page.

Virtually every story can be told in less than two, double-spaced pages. If your draft runs longer, edit the release down. Identify the end with either "--30--" or "####." This tells the editor that there are no more pages to your story.

Proofread and correct your text, then reproduce it using a machine that makes clear copies. A photocopier is best, but a well-maintained mimeograph machine can be a tolerable substitute. Staple and fold the release neatly, then mail or hand deliver as required. Have it hand carried by a volunteer or mail it special delivery if there is any possibility that you will miss an outlet's deadline.

Follow up with a phone call to make sure your release reached the right reporter or editor and to answer any questions. This double-check gives you a personal opportunity to "sell" the story. It's also a chance to add any last-minute facts or new angles. If volunteers assist you in making these calls, be sure they are well-briefed and have a prepared script.

Finally, file a number of copies of the release in headquarters for use in answering questions and creating press kits.

A sample candidate's announcement release appears on page 125.

★ **Diane**
Walters
for
Senator

For Information Contact:

Spokesperson *### - ####*

(home)   *### - ####*

For release at 2:00 p.m., Thursday, May 20, 1986

DIANE WALTERS LAUNCHES "RESPONSIVE" CAMPAIGN FOR STATE SENATE

Hometown Human Services Director Diane Walters today announced her candidacy for the 5th District State Senate seat.

Ms. Walters declared, "For too long our community has been ignored by the people who are supposed to be representing us. We need someone more responsive to the district's needs. I intend to fight for such vital services as a new senior citizens' center, expanded day care, and an effective consumer protection agency."

"The problem is that too many incumbents care more about the concerns of professional lobbyists than about the needs of their constituents," Ms. Walters charged. "I won't be another of the boys on capitol hill. I know that state government can be made to work better."

Ms. Walters has been the Director of Human Services since 1976. She is also a member of the area Mental Health Advisory Board, a trustee of a local Children's Center, and a regular volunteer at the senior center.

"Through my work and community service activities I've had the opportunity to meet many Hometown residents and learn their concerns," Ms. Walters continued. "During the course of the campaign I plan to go door-to-door to hear what voters need from their State Senator. Anyone with questions about my positions should feel free to give me a call at any time. That's the open and accessible way I intend to run my campaign and my Senate office."

Along with her husband, Richard, an engineer, Ms. Walters lives at 1927 Constitution Avenue. They have two children, Lisa and John, who attend Kennedy Elementary School.

— 30 —

Press Kits

Reporters and editors will often seek background material about a candidate and the campaign. Creating a standard press kit is a simple way to meet this demand.

★ **Diane**
Walters
for
Senator

For Information Contact:

Spokesperson ###.####

Telephone ###.####

For Immediate Release

LOCAL TENANTS GROUP ENDORSES WALTERS FOR STATE SENATE

The Hometown Tenants Organization has voted to back Diane Walter's candidacy for the 5th District State Senate seat. The endorsement was made at the group's regular monthly meeting at the Elks Hall on Tuesday evening.

According to Jonathan King, the organization's chairman, "Our 450 members believe that Diane Walters will best serve the interests of women and men in Hometown who rent their homes and apartments. She will work for programs like fuel assistance and home repair loans that help both tenants and homeowners." Prior to its decision the tenants group sent a detailed questionnaire to all candidates concerning their positions on housing issues.

Ms. Walters thanked the group for its endorsement in a telegram sent Wednesday morning. "I am most grateful for the help of the Hometown Tenants Organization and all the other local community leaders who are supporting my campaign. Working together we can build a state government that will be more responsive to all our needs."

The Walters campaign, headquartered at 1927 Constitution Avenue, has also received endorsements from local taxpayers and environmental groups. Ms. Walters will appear at a campaign forum this Saturday night before the League of Women Voters.

— 30 —

The press kit should contain a biographical sketch of your candidate, a fact sheet on policy positions with brief quotations on key issues, a list of names and phone numbers of campaign staff who are authorized to speak to the media, samples of campaign materials such as a brochure and bumper sticker and copies of a few favorable news clippings. Throughout the course of the cam-

126

paign, add news releases on such topics as key endorsements and major policy statements.

Don't forget to include pictures. One candidate for county commissioner who failed to provide the local media with a current photograph found that a prominent weekly paper illustrated a front-page campaign story with a file photo of his opponent. For print media a 5 x 7 or 8 x 10 glossy, black-and-white photo portrait of the candidate should be included. Television stations will want a matte-finished print or a 35mm color slide.

Some campaigns may wish to enclose even more in the press kit. Optional items include biographies of family members and top campaign staff, "candid" photos of the candidate, contribution records and letters of support from well-known individuals and groups. The precise content of the kit will depend on the information the campaign wishes to stress as well as the demands of the local media. Just make sure each item is consistent with your campaign's basic theme.

All this material should be packaged neatly in a folder or large envelope. A supply of kits should always be kept at headquarters where they can be revised as information changes and new releases added.

Photos

In addition to their use in press kits, photographs offer another tool for obtaining press coverage. Even if pictures are not worth a thousand words each, they are attractive to television and print editors because they offer a visual alternative to a sea of written or spoken words. For small papers especially, they are a low-cost way to fill space.

Photos can accompany campaign releases or be sent out alone. Either way, every photograph should have a caption attached. Never write on the back of a picture—the pressure of your pen can crack the surface and make reproduction difficult. Instead, type the caption on a sheet of plain paper and tape it to the bottom of the print. In one or two sentences the caption should identify the people and place shown, the date of the event, and explain the story behind the picture.

Find out photo requirements of each outlet when you conduct your initial media outlet survey. Some outlets prefer to take their own photographs. Don't waste your time and the campaign's money printing and mailing unsolicited pictures where there is no chance they will be used. Also, find out photo deadlines; they may differ from those of news stories.

Radio Actualities

Many radio stations are willing to air brief, taped statements issued by your candidate as part of their regular news broadcasts. These are called "actualities." The campaign's job is to record the segments and transmit them to receptive stations in a technically acceptable manner.

The first task is taping a statement that highlights a story editors will view as newsworthy. Most stations will not use anything that runs over thirty seconds because radio news broadcasts rarely last more than five minutes. Again, newsworthiness is always a subjective judgment, but stories that react to the day's news events are more likely to be aired than those that simply state your candidate's position on an issue.

Obviously, the recorded segment should be free of confusing noises. Some background sounds that convey an impression of being "on the scene" are useful, but not if they obscure the candidate's voice. Either record "live" by having your candidate speak extemporaneously or have him or her read the most interesting paragraph of the release.

You must then prepare the actuality for transmission. At the beginning of the tape, preceding the candidate's statement, record an identification of the speaker, the time length (in seconds) of the statement, and a short background statement about the story. Follow this with a countdown "5-4-3-2-1" that cues the start of the actuality. Most of this information can be put on tape prior to recording the candidate's statement. An accurate time count can be added later. Alternatively, a statement selected from a prerecorded speech can be edited in after the cuing information by using two tape recorders.

Here's how the final version would be transcribed: "Today, local Human Services Director Diane Walters kicked off her campaign for the 8th District state senate seat. Twenty-two seconds. 5-4-3-2-1. . . ."

Once the actuality is recorded, the press secretary or a trained volunteer calls the radio stations, asks if they are interested in the story, and then plays the tape. If your recorder has a tone control, turn it all the way to the treble position before feeding the actuality. This will make the transmission crisp and clear. Too much bass will make the sound "muddy."

Many local telephone companies and electronics stores sell equipment designed to help transmit actualities. A common version "couples" a tape recorder to the telephone line so that sound can be fed without any loss in quality. A simpler and cheaper method is to wire the output jack of a cassette recorder to the two brass prongs revealed when you unscrew a standard telephone mouthpiece and lift out the microphone. Shops for electronics hobbyists, such as Radio Shack, will sell you the appropriate connecting device if you ask for "two alligator clips on a cord." The choice of technology should depend on the campaign's media budget and the number of actualities you are likely to transmit. The most sophisticated voice couplers cost several hundred dollars; the simple wire connections less than five.

It is not necessary to call all the stations on your list every time the candidate issues a statement. If the story primarily concerns one geographic area, you should contact only those stations which reach that target audience. For example, a farm story should be sent only to the radio outlets serving the rural parts of your district.

Media Events

It's hard to generate much news coverage for the day-to-day activities of a local race. Door-to-door canvassing and fundraising will seldom spark a reporter's interest. If media coverage is essential for delivering your campaign's message and increasing the candidate's visibility, you may have to create special events that spark the media's interest in order to get coverage.

Preparation is always required to get reporters to attend any campaign activity. Assignment editors must be notified, press kits and releases prepared, and space set aside for reporters, cameras, and recording gear. Details about the event's location, travel directions, and access must be provided. The media must know precisely what time your candidate's speech or other newsworthy story will occur.

Always make reminder calls to confirm details and sell your story. The best time to call for a morning event is the previous afternoon. If your event is in the afternoon, call early in the morning of the same day.

Action-oriented events stand a better chance of drawing media coverage. Greeting workers at the plant gate or on the shop floor provides more interesting visual and sound images than standing at a podium in a union hall. Some of these activities have become trite from overuse, so be creative in designing unusual events that tie in with your basic themes and the concerns of your target audience. Your candidate's statement on utility rates released at a meeting with low-income senior citizens who are threatened with shut-offs will receive more attention than the same position paper circulated at some other time. Organize the events to provide good photo opportunities. Remember to have copies of statements, releases, fact sheets, and the like available for reporters. And never charge working reporters an admission fee to any campaign activity they are covering, even a fundraiser.

The press secretary should work closely with the candidate's scheduler to identify events that can be effectively publicized. You want to take full advantage of every chance to obtain news coverage.

News Conferences

A news conference is an event designed solely for media coverage. Since it provides a controlled environment set up to meet their needs, more reporters are likely to cover a story if there's a news conference than if a release is simply mailed out. A news conference also gives the candidate an opportunity to explain a complex issue in greater depth than is possible in a printed release.

However, be careful! News conferences also present risks. Reporters at a news conference may feel peer pressure to ask tough questions that would not be posed if the same information were presented through a release or in a campaign speech. The candidate and other speakers must be prepared with simple, comprehensible responses. Otherwise, the media may focus on the candidate's unprepared or inarticulate answers rather than on the well-rehearsed statement.

As a result, news conferences should only be called when the campaign has a major announcement to make or important news to break. Don't get the reputation of calling a news conference once a week for trivial stories. And don't even bother calling one in a district with only a handful of news outlets. In that case, it's easier to schedule individual interviews with the right reporters.

Members of the media should always be informed of a planned news conference at least three to four days in advance. One effective technique is to send an initial notice in the form of a news release or a media advisory like the one on page 132, which outlines the date, time, place, and basic content of the announcement. Follow up with phone calls to the most important outlets as you would for any event. Notify all major outlets and every reporter who has covered your campaign in order to avoid accusations of favoritism.

Take care to schedule the news conference so it does not conflict with other news events. It's best to make a few calls before formally announcing the event to ensure that the reporters you want are available at the proposed time. Don't spend time making arrangements only to discover that key journalists have conflicts. Consider reporters' deadlines, too. The most convenient times are usually between 10 A.M. and 2 P.M. Mondays and Tuesdays are best for reaching weekly papers that often come out on Thursdays and Fridays. Again, your initial media outlet survey will reveal which days and times are best in your area.

A suitable location must be chosen. There should be adequate space for cameras and reporters, a lectern or table on which to place microphones, and a pleasant visual backdrop. Be certain there are sufficient electrical outlets to plug in lights and other equipment. Arrange for extension cords if plugs are located far from where your speakers will stand. Ask a friendly reporter for advice if you are unsure of the media's technical requirements.

Before the event, prepare a written release summarizing the information to be presented at the news conference as well as copies of the candidate's statement to distribute to reporters as they arrive. Have a sign-up sheet to record the names and affiliations of all those in attendance. All speakers should be briefed and answers to likely questions rehearsed. Have appropriate pictures and statistics available as back-up documentation.

Start the news conference promptly. The candidate should open with a statement no more than two or three minutes in length. Then the people who will provide supporting statements should speak briefly. Optionally, a prominent person making an endorsement can speak first, followed by the candidate.

★ **Diane
Walters
for
Senator**

For Information Contact:

Spokesperson ### - ####
(home)   ### - ####

MEDIA ADVISORY

WHAT: Announcement of Housing Plan to eliminate waiting
          lists for Senior Citizens' Apartments in Hometown.

WHEN: Tuesday, September 11
          2:00 p.m.

WHERE: Community Room
          Hometown Senior Housing Center
          1234 Main Street

WHO: Diane Walters, candidate for State Senate
          Mary Jones, President, Seniors for Adequate Housing
          John Jeffords, United Community Housing Corp.

WHY: Over 200 Hometown senior citizens are on waiting lists
          for apartments in the town's one elderly housing
          development. The waiting period for a vacancy runs
          from five to seven years. Hometown has fewer senior
          housing units per capita than any community in the
          county.

Note: To reach the Community Room take the elevator in the
west tower of the Senior Housing Center to the third floor.

Never schedule more than two or three spokespeople. There's no way a single story can do justice to the information a larger group tries to present. After opening statements are completed, ask for questions. When questioning slows down or after about thirty minutes end the news conference by thanking everyone. Don't let the event drag on until reporters become bored. It's always better to leave a few questions unanswered than to have minutes of awkward silence.

Afterward, the candidate should remain to mingle with re-porters and respond to additional questions or requests for indi-vidual interviews. The release and the candidate's statement should be hand-delivered to reporters who were unable to attend. You may also want to try to set up phone interviews or transmit taped actualities to key outlets that missed the event.

Opportunities for Free Coverage

As your media outlet survey should have indicated, every district is served by a variety of communications channels that reach your target audience. The five most widespread vehicles for campaign media are:

- Television
- Radio
- Daily newspapers
- Weeklies
- Special interest publications

Each of these vehicles presents opportunities for free coverage. Plan carefully to determine how each one can be used in your campaign and which "tools of the trade" will be most effective for winning access.

Television

Television is the primary source of information for adults who fol-low political news. No other communications vehicle compares with television for conveying action and intensity. And it is the only medium that can reinforce your message with pictures, sound, and the printed word. Because TV most closely approxi-mates one-to-one contact, it is the most persuasive media available to communicate a campaign message.

Naturally, competition for TV coverage is intense. Getting access for a local campaign is especially hard. If you are successful at all, your day in the sun may be no more than a fifteen-second clip. Many television outlets simply ignore local races because the station's service area includes a large number of districts. Assignment editors believe most viewers will not be interested in stories about candidates for whom they cannot vote.

Even in the unusual cases where your district roughly coincides with a station's service area, it's still not easy to get TV time. The typical half-hour, locally produced news show has only ten to fifteen minutes to cover all the day's major stories. The rest of the time is devoted to sports, weather, features, and commercials.

If TV news coverage is a real possibility in your race, be sure that your news conferences and other events are designed for the medium. The key is to think visually. Action is necessary because TV is based on moving pictures. The setting must reinforce the spoken words to hold the viewer's attention. Statements for TV must be especially brief. Typical news stories run sixty to ninety seconds and include comments by the reporter and anchor—that allows time for less than two hundred words. Therefore, the candidate must make the main points in one or two sentences. This takes practice. Decide in advance what the message is and hone it down to a short, quotable phrase.

Since TV reporters, their technical crews, and equipment represent expensive investments, station managers want each team to cover several stories a day. As a result, events held close to the station are more likely to be covered because they require far less nonproductive travel time.

Aside from regularly scheduled news broadcasts, television offers few other opportunities for local campaign coverage. On some occasions, stations present candidate forums or debates, but these are rarely scheduled during prime viewing time. Talk shows and "Meet the Press"–style interviews have potential, but producers may shy away from candidates because of the equal opportunity requirement that all other candidates for the same office be afforded airtime. To inquire about access, write to the show's producer and then follow up with a phone call. But remember that you may be creating a showcase for a lesser known or more photogenic opponent.

All these decisions should be guided by your overall campaign strategy. Generally, a well-known incumbent will not want to give an opponent free time, but most challengers should not turn down opportunities.

In about a third of all communities, cable television systems provide additional channels for reaching potential viewers. Many local producers are eager for stories or guests who will give legitimacy to their relatively new medium.

Although extensive public service programming provides many opportunities for coverage, cable is still in its developmental stage. In fact, more viewers subscribe to cable to improve their reception of remote channels than to watch the cable system's own programs. Your campaign may find it necessary to do extensive contacting of supporters to build an audience to watch the candidate's appearance. For example, you may want to plan a number of simultaneous fundraising parties to coincide with a cable show featuring your candidate.

Keep in mind that the probability of reaching significant numbers of persuadable voters is small. Before pursuing cable programming, make sure the expected payoff is likely to justify the time invested.

Radio

There are more opportunities to reach your target audience with radio. While TV stations usually serve large metropolitan areas, most radio outlets serve only a few towns. Others aim their programming at particular demographic groups, such as students, farmers, minorities, or senior citizens. Your media survey will tell you which outlets are most appropriate for your campaign.

Actualities and news releases are the best techniques for access to regular newscasts. Though there are only a few minutes available each hour, radio news directors are always looking for lively local stories. Usually, they are very receptive to candidates who are willing to come to the studio for interviews. Some stations like to explore issues in depth in a news series or public affairs show. Though they may prefer to seek out candidates, there is no harm in calling or writing to suggest a programming idea.

Many radio outlets also produce forums or debates. Access is obtained by contacting the station and finding out what formats are available.

Free airtime may also be available on call-in talk shows. Your candidate can appear as a guest so long as the station devotes equal amounts of programming to other candidates. Calls from supporters who phone in comments about your candidate make this format even more effective. The press secretary may want to arrange for volunteers to call in regularly to the most popular shows to praise your candidate and to question your opponent's positions and record. Make certain volunteers are well-prepared to speak persuasively about your campaign.

Many stations also offer special programs for groups of listeners who may be among your campaign's target audiences. By participating in farm or business reports, ethnic music and cultural shows, and foreign language broadcasts, your candidate can speak directly to key groups. Or you may want to arrange for a supporter from one of these groups to represent the campaign. Again, the route of access to these special programs involves personal contact with individual producers at each station.

Some radio and television stations endorse candidates. Find out which ones do and how they decide when you conduct your initial media survey. Then make sure the appropriate editorial directors are on your list for regular news releases and candidate visits. Remember, too, that supporters of non-endorsed candidates must be allowed to rebut the station's editorial stand.

Daily Newspapers

Virtually every page in the paper presents an opportunity for coverage of some facet of the campaign, even in the smallest-circulation daily. Though most print media do not have nearly the reach or impact of major electronic outlets, they are still followed closely by opinion leaders and the most likely voters.

Nearly all the tools discussed in this chapter can be used to get newspaper coverage. Releases can translate into news stories. Photographs can be directly reproduced by the paper. Press kits can help persuade editors to provide more frequent and accurate stories about your candidate.

In addition to news stories, the campaign can promote coverage by dealing directly with the staff of different sections of the newspaper. Certain writers are responsible for feature stories that explore human interest angles. Individual reporters or their editors can be approached with a letter, phone call, or personal visit suggesting a likely topic. A Wisconsin candidate virtually locked up the senior citizen vote in her local race with a full-page story about the seventy-year-old volunteer who was running her campaign office. The quotes from the volunteer and pictures showing her in the office surrounded by campaign signs delivered a very persuasive message.

Written background information should be provided by your campaign, but the substance and style of the article are usually out of your control. Remember, the writer's interests are not the same as your campaign's. You must carefully consider whether a feature story will accurately project your message. One campaign press secretary worked hard to place a story about the candidate, a highly qualified professional woman, in the Home/Living section of the local metropolitan daily. The angle the campaign expected to have covered was how a mother of four successfully balanced her family and community obligations while running for public office. The resulting story, however, depicted the candidate as "Dotty Domestic," better suited to being a den mother than an elected official.

Women who are first-time candidates or challengers may face an especially hard time establishing their credentials. Questions of competence often pose obstacles not faced by their male counterparts. Consider whether this will be a problem when designing your campaign theme. Structure news releases in such a way as to get feature stories that reinforce *your* message.

If you decide a feature story would help deliver your campaign message, identify the most appropriate reporter by looking at the bylines on articles of a similar nature. You can reduce your risk of a negative story by seeking out someone whose views already seem sympathetic.

Political reporters may also be open to your ideas for columns. The day-to-day events of the campaign can provide a good starting point for more in-depth analysis of a complex issue or an exploration of your candidate's strategy. Personal contact, especially by the candidate, campaign manager, or press secretary, is the best way to offer suggestions and provide information. Again, scanning the newspaper will reveal the most appropriate outlets.

The campaign should have a separate strategy for seeking editorials. Many papers endorse candidates, and some push very strongly for their choices. Since the individuals who make editorial decisions are usually not the people who cover news, you must deal with them separately from your regular contacts with reporters. On some papers, the owner or publisher controls the endorsements.

It helps for the candidate to personally visit editorial decision-makers early in the campaign and then maintain the relationship by occasionally delivering major statements and releases in person. If you don't know whether a newspaper plans to endorse a candidate in your race, ask. An editorial that falls short of full-scale support can still help if it treats your candidate favorably. When you receive an endorsement or positive mention, disseminate it widely by clipping and reproducing the material. The candidate should personally thank the editors for their support.

The "Letters to the Editor" column is among the most heavily read parts of the newspaper. It's a perfect place for the campaign to respond officially to criticism or elaborate on a news story. Even better are "unsolicited" letters from grass-roots supporters pointing out the candidate's accomplishments and issue positions. These personal endorsements often carry more weight with readers than the views expressed in editorial columns.

Follow the basic rules for writing news releases in drafting letters. A bit more opinion is acceptable, but don't become heavy-handed. Always be brief, factual, and lively. Pay attention to any guidelines the paper has printed concerning maximum length and submission deadlines. Your campaign can help generate letters, but each one must be individually written and signed by a real supporter. Many papers check the legitimacy of signatures by calling the supposed author, and editors automatically discard obvious form letters.

A sample campaign Letter to the Editor appears on page 139.

Weeklies

On a smaller scale, local weekly papers offer the same opportunities for coverage as the metropolitan dailies. More so than most dailies, they will cover local races. In fact, since weeklies have fewer reporters and smaller budgets, their editors will often print well-written campaign releases that include an interesting angle for local readers. Weekly newspaper reporters respond especially well to a personal touch. A visit by your candidate is likely to result in a favorable story and a photograph.

September 30, 1985

TO THE EDITOR:

This fall, Hometown residents have an opportunity to vote

for a candidate who understands our community's need for

vital services like a new senior citizens' center, expanded day care,

and tougher consumer protection.

Diane Walters, who is running for the State Senate seat,

is committed to making government work for the taxpayer. As

local Human Services head, Ms. Walters was an outstanding

administrator who always delivered first-rate programs within

her budget.

All of us who have worked with her believe Diane Walters

would be a most effective advocate for Hometown interests at

the state capital. We've joined together as Volunteers for

Walters (150 Main Street, 555-3456), and urge everyone who

thinks we need a strong senator to join us by working for

Diane now and voting for her in November.

Sincerely,

Mary Thomson
North Street

Similarly, weekly newspaper columnists, editorial writers, and feature reporters may appreciate the opportunity to interview a candidate or sit down for an hour with the campaign manager. Local Letters to the Editor are studied intensely to see which townspeople are lined up behind which candidate. Even social gossip columns are looking for items to publish; let the writers know the names of community coordinators and local hosts of campaign fundraising events.

Special Interest Publications

Nearly every special interest group in your district will have its own publication. Though they rarely reach beyond the group's membership, newsletters and bulletins are read attentively within the small circles in which they circulate. Stories about the candidate can be especially persuasive when printed in a publication with which the reader closely identifies.

General releases that may be of interest to one of your campaign's target audiences should be sent to all the publications serving that constituency. It's especially important to seek coverage in publications put out by organizations that have endorsed your candidacy. In addition, the campaign may put out a special release designed for inclusion in community group newsletters, senior citizens' bulletins, and the like.

Your Legal Rights to Coverage

Many candidates and their workers enter a campaign assuming they will automatically get media coverage. Some people even believe they have a Constitutional right to access. Except in very limited circumstances, these notions are totally false.

Every outlet, both print and electronic, has almost total discretion over what is included in news stories. In effect, editors may decide that your campaign does not merit coverage because your candidate is not "serious." Fortunately, most media decision-makers use this power with some discretion. But no campaign should ever base its strategy on the presumption that it will achieve the media coverage it desires.

The few laws governing the media and campaigns are vague and extremely complex. The explanations that follow provide an overview of equal opportunity, print media access limitations, libel, and slander. Review these to understand the basic rules, but be prepared to consult an attorney specializing in media law if a problem arises.

Equal Opportunity in Radio and Television

Only on radio and television does a candidate have anything approaching a legal right to coverage. Since broadcast laws are based on the principle that the public owns the airwaves, the Federal Communications Commission (FCC) has mandated certain conditions for granting licenses. One of these is the Equal Opportunity Requirement, sometimes wrongly called "Equal Time."

Basically, Equal Opportunity compels every station to treat all candidates for the same office identically with respect to coverage outside regular news broadcasts. If one candidate is allowed to purchase advertising time, every contender in the same race must be offered the opportunity to purchase the same amount of time for the same price. If your opponent appears on radio or TV in a nonnews format such as extended coverage of a campaign speech or as a guest on an interview show, the station is obligated to make the same amount of coverage at the same time in the programming day available to your candidate without charge. Candidates also have a right to respond to editorials in which station management endorses an opponent.

To encourage enforcement of the Equal Opportunity Requirement, the FCC has laid out certain guidelines. Every station must disclose how much each campaign has spent to purchase commercials and the precise time they will be run. Stations are also barred from trying to freeze out all but the richest candidate by charging extremely high rates. If they are sold at all, political commercials must be billed to all campaigns at the lowest rate available to any commercial advertiser. The station may not censor your political advertising in any way; they cannot refuse to run a spot or ask you to change wording, even to eliminate obscenity.

Of course, these rules do nothing to help your campaign if it cannot afford advertising at any price. Nor do they have any effect in a race where a station refuses to sell time to all candidates. Your initial outlet survey should identify every station's policy about political advertising.

Access to Print Media

While the public theoretically owns the airwaves and "rents" them to private broadcasters, the law is clear that individual companies own newspapers. The First Amendment to the U.S. Constitution prohibits any laws that regulate what newspapers may print. As a result there are no equivalent protections governing your campaign's access to print media.

Newspapers are not required to sell space to your candidate in any circumstance, nor are they required to disclose your opponent's purchases. They can refuse to accept all advertising, selectively accept ads for one candidate, or require heavy editing of your copy before they will print it. They can even charge competing candidates different rates.

Similarly, there's no obligation for newspapers to cover your news stories. Especially on small papers, there's a tendency to blatant partisanship. After a photograph of an opposing candidate appeared with a front-page news story, one suburban publisher even sent a memo to his staff warning, "It's not our policy to give free publicity to the enemy." The candidate, whose picture never again appeared in that paper, had no legal recourse.

Financial considerations and good community relations may inhibit the most outrageous practices, but there have been cases of blatant discrimination against some campaigns.

Libel and Slander

A candidate also has little protection from personal attacks or false charges in the media. It is almost impossible for a candidate to recover any damages on the grounds that a printed story in a newspaper constitutes libel or that an oral statement by a broadcaster is slander.

Courts have repeatedly held that "public figures" including candidates must demonstrate that the person who uttered the defamatory remarks knew they were false or didn't care about their truthfulness and consciously intended to harm the candidate. Since it is usually possible for a defendant to claim that the charge appeared true at the time, successful court challenges by candidates are rare. Moreover, some judges have held that the campaign process already offers ample opportunities to counter false statements.

This does not mean that your campaign should not react politically to false attacks. Simply don't depend on legal remedies.

Monitoring

Careful observation of major local outlets is required to assess the effectiveness of your campaign's media plans. If possible, reliable volunteers or a commercial clipping service should read all district newspapers and watch or listen to all major newscasts.

Monitoring provides feedback about the impact of individual releases, news conferences, and media events. It also gathers vital information about the opponent's activities and media plans.

Optimally, newspaper stories, columns, and editorials about all the candidates in your race should be clipped and broadcast news items recorded and timed. All the information about coverage should be added to the media survey sheet for each outlet. The data can then be analyzed to evaluate the value of particular tactics. If your press conferences do not result in as many stories as other events, it makes sense to alter the media plan.

The campaign leadership should look for other patterns in the coverage. If a media outlet or reporter can be shown to have given another candidate more favorable coverage, it is possible to seek corrective action. Most editors want to be fair, even if they are bound by few legal requirements. If bias can be factually demonstrated with clipping files and time charts, they are likely to try to restore balance.

Should a station broadcast an editorial, personal attack, or advertisement subject to the Equal Opportunity Requirement, monitoring will give you an early warning and yield more time to prepare a response. Your campaign will also be able to counter an unfavorable news story more rapidly or react to an opponent's claims while the issue is still timely. Often a phone call from the candidate or campaign manager will result in your side of the story appearing on subsequent broadcasts.

Monitoring can also alert the campaign to new issues as they develop in the district. Local call-in shows and "Letters to the Editor" columns are among the first places problems are mentioned.

This type of feedback is important for keeping your media work on track. Even if you don't make perfect decisions the first time you write your media plan, monitoring will help you learn from your successes and failures.

7

PAID MEDIA

Many campaign workers assume that an article about their candidate in the newspaper or a story on the local news show reaches most potential voters. But research indicates that only 15 to 20 percent of all adults in the nation are plugged into the news in any meaningful manner—and this figure includes all forms of delivery. In some media markets, the TV evening news actually has a smaller audience than such shows as "I Love Lucy" and "Bowling for Dollars." And many newspaper subscribers read only the comics and sports pages.

The campaign is even at a disadvantage with the minority of voters who are attentive to free media. In most news or public affairs formats, both the content and placement of your message is beyond your control. Even though they receive your news releases, news outlets may misreport, edit, or totally eliminate the crucial part of your message.

Paid media presents no such risks; for a price, your campaign can be in full control of both message and audience. Just like field and candidate contact activities, advertising allows your campaign to repetitively deliver *your* message, in *your* own words, to reach *your* particular target audience. No one can edit your radio and television advertising or campaign leaflets in any manner. Newspaper or billboard sales staffs may insist on changes before an ad is run, but your campaign always has the power to withdraw the advertising. There's no way your message can be distorted.

Paid media has only one drawback, yet it is a big one for the low-budget campaign: advertising requires money—often lots of it. And cash is a resource that is usually in short supply. Volunteer time can substitute for money in most every other part of your campaign, from delivering literature door-to-door instead of by mail to calling reporters from home instead of the campaign headquarters' phone. With advertising, however, the rule is cash-in-advance. There's no form of in-kind payment that most outlets will accept.

As a result, the real limit on the use of paid media in your campaign will be your basic budget. For many local candidates, advertising will be the single biggest line-item since even a handful of spots can cost several thousand dollars. But that allocation of scarce resources may make sense if your campaign plan determines that paid media is essential to reinforce the delivery of your message to target voters at a critical time.

Advertising Specialists

If your campaign plan includes a role for paid media, you should use advertising specialists to ensure that you get the most impact for your media dollars. Creating a thirty-second spot or half-page newspaper ad is entirely different from any other form of writing. Every word and every pause has to carry meaning. It takes a lot of talent and experience to translate something as complicated as a political campaign theme into a brief advertisement.

The quality of the presentation is as important as the content of the message in influencing voters. The typical local candidate will drop everything to get a news story in a small weekly newspaper. Yet the same campaign will usually allow an office volunteer to design a leaflet and budget only an afternoon for recording its radio spots. Such priorities are unwise. A well-designed spot or leaflet is probably more important than one weekly newspaper story because the advertising delivers your message to a larger audience more effectively.

If the radio spot has a great message but sounds garbled, it's not going to win many voters. And if the leaflet presents compelling arguments hidden in a cluttered format, there's less chance that potential voters will be persuaded. Advertising specialists have the skills and training needed to make accurate design judgments.

We don't purport to train you to do your own advertising production. Rather, we want to give you the information you will need to make better use of the services of professionals whether they are paid consultants or experienced volunteers.

Professional services may be purchased from any advertising firm, but make sure the agency has a track record of success in political work. Before you hire anyone, see if you can get help from qualified volunteers. Check out staff from local community groups that have run effective communications programs. College public relations, arts, and journalism programs are other good sources for free or low-cost help. Many students have to complete a practical internship as a requirement for graduation. Since their work is supervised by professors who often have worked in advertising, the quality can be quite high. Or ask teachers you know to contribute their talents to the campaign directly.

It is also possible to mix volunteer and professional services. You can produce a radio spot very inexpensively by having an experienced volunteer write the copy. An announcer's time and production assistance can then be purchased from a local station. This is the way many commercial advertisers produce spots in small towns.

The Paid Media Plan

Once your campaign has decided upon its basic message and overall advertising budget, it must answer four specific questions to design its paid media plan:

- What outlets are the most cost-effective vehicles to reach your target audience?

- What types of media will your target audience find most persuasive?

- How should the content of your message be designed for paid media?

- When is the best time for your advertising to be aired, published, or distributed?

Your professional advertising specialist will help you think through these questions in the context of your district. But you should understand certain basic principles and concepts.

Cost-Effectiveness

Various means of delivering a paid message should be evaluated in terms of the financial investment needed to reach each voter. This is called "cost-effectiveness."

When you begin to assess media cost-effectiveness, it is likely you will encounter some misconceptions. Many people assume that direct mail or leaflets are always cheapest because of their low unit costs, while TV and radio are comparatively expensive. Yet just the opposite is often the case.

For example, it costs at least two to three cents per copy to produce a piece of printed literature in quantity. You simply cannot get decent design and production for much less. For comparison, assume that each leaflet will be read by one potential voter. Some will be thrown away, others will be passed on to family members, but on the average one leaflet equals one impression. At two to three cents each, you get about thirty to fifty impressions for every dollar.

Now consider direct mail. A well-packaged solicitation sent at bulk rates can't be designed, printed, and mailed for much less than twenty cents apiece. Making the assumption that each letter reaches one voter, you discover that one dollar buys you around five impressions.

Though advertising prices and circulations vary greatly, daily newspapers generally deliver fifty to a hundred impressions per dollar spent on full-page advertising. Buying half pages would seem to double these figures, but more readers will overlook your ad the smaller it gets. The cost-effectiveness of weekly newspapers falls into the same general range.

The highest audience-to-costs ratios can be achieved through television and radio. Figures as high as 400 to 500 impressions per dollar are not unusual, but they are deceptive. The reason is that the coverage area, or media market, served by local broadcast outlets is usually much larger than your electoral district.

To get more meaningful data, the initial cost-effectiveness numbers must be adjusted to reflect the *net* impressions per dollar.

This calculation involves reducing the total audience figure by a fraction reflecting the percentage of the outlet's coverage area in your district. If a radio station serves four equal-sized districts, the overall ratio of 400 to 500 impressions per dollar drops to one-quarter of that figure, or about 100 to 125 net impressions per dollar for your target audience. In this case, radio would still be your most cost-effective medium. But if the same station served ten districts, the net cost-effectiveness ratio would range between forty and fifty impressions per dollar, probably worse than the local weekly paper. Of course, raw data for newspapers that cover more than one district must also be adjusted.

Other costs enter into the equation. Although radio and TV charge about the same per impression for airtime, creating and taping a professionally announced radio spot costs several hundred dollars while a TV ad of like quality costs ten times more. Radio spots can also be revised in a couple of hours. Such differences in production expenses must be considered in determining the most efficient use of the media.

Cost-effectiveness is not a precise measure, but it is a useful tool for making initial judgments about the best way to reach potential voters.

Target Audience

Paid media can be used to reach both large and smaller, specialized constituencies. Your campaign's media survey will have identified the outlets that most effectively reach each target audience. For example, if you want to attract commuting workers, radio spots can be purchased during "drive time", or billboards can be purchased along major roadways. Similarly, advertising can be purchased in specialized publications that appeal to other demographic groups.

There are many cases in which the campaign's targeting demands outweigh general considerations of cost-effectiveness. If senior citizens are a key constituency in your district and you can readily extract from voter registration data a list of everyone over sixty-five, then direct mail makes sense. Computers make it possible to do very specialized direct mailing without lots of staff time. Even the extra costs of the computer run and postage may be justified if reaching this group is a high priority for your campaign.

For similar reasons, special-interest publications such as labor newspapers may be the best buy to reach union members even if the advertising cost per reader seems high. This is especially true if there are no other media in your district that reach the particular target audience.

Among the electronic media, radio allows more effective targeting than television. This is because most people tune in consistently to one or two radio stations. Listeners do not frequently spin the dial in search of a particular radio show. The opposite is true of TV. Individuals watch specific programs and regularly switch from channel to channel.

Radio stations with different formats can be used to select audiences with particular demographic characteristics. Individuals with college degrees are more likely to listen to classical music than people with less formal education. More blue-collar workers tune in the country and western stations than folk music. These divisions are not absolute, but comparatively each format does draw a unique audience.

Much less targeting can be done with TV. More senior citizens watch "The Lawrence Welk Show" while "Saturday Night Live" draws a much higher percentage of young adults. But most television shows, especially those broadcast during prime time, are designed to appeal to the largest possible audience. As a result, TV shows are usually viewed by a broad range of demographic groups. This eliminates most opportunities for targeting.

Data about station demographics is relatively easy to obtain. Every station has precise numbers available because that is what they use to sell commercial advertising. Ad agencies and media buyers also have access to the same figures. If you're going to try targeting without professional help, business school libraries may have the current Nielsen and Arbitron surveys on file in the reference section. These books will provide the station's demographics for every hour of the day.

Content

The more homogeneous the audience, the more specific the message can be. A letter sent only to senior citizens, an advertising spot on a Spanish-language program, or an ad in a union newspaper can address only the concerns of that group. On the other hand, a commercial aired during a prime-time television show must appeal to a broad audience. For most people, a more specific message is more persuasive.

Some messages work best in one particular type of media. Radio and TV are not particularly effective for delivering factual information, but they are very good at conveying emotion. The opposite is true of print. If your message is logical, look to newspapers, direct mail, or leaflets where you can list arguments or develop issues. Radio is good for creating general images since people usually listen to it as background while they perform other activities. TV is the most powerful emotionally because it directly engages the viewer and can reinforce a message with pictures, speech, and written words.

In some cases, the message will have to be designed to mesh with the chosen medium. If radio is the most cost-effective medium in your district then the message should probably be grounded in emotion rather than logic. A radio ad shouldn't overwhelm the audience with a list of your qualifications for office. Instead, it should develop a simple theme, like "honesty" or "experience."

This is not to suggest that an emotional message can't be conveyed in newspapers or campaign literature. It's just that the electronic media are better suited. Whether you begin by choosing a medium because of cost-effectiveness or start with the message due to other considerations, the distinction between emotion and logic remains critical.

Timing

When purchasing advertising, buy backward from Election Day. People are more attentive to campaign messages just before they vote. The first priority for your paid media should be to buy this most important time. Your advertising should reach a peak at the same time your other direct and indirect voter contact activities are most intense. This is the best way to repetitively deliver your message.

Statewide and national campaigns often heed consultant Joe Napolitan's adage, "Dominate the dominant medium." Increasingly, for presidential campaigns, that means concentrating spending on television. Even for congressional races, it is not unusual to spend half the entire campaign budget on TV advertising.

But for high-volunteer, low-budget campaigns that ratio makes no sense. It's more effective to spend the bulk of your money on the materials the candidate and campaign workers need to contact voters individually.

Certain techniques can stretch the modest advertising budget that may be left after direct voter contact. A campaign that can't afford to advertise continuously for two months can purchase some early time and space to establish name recognition. Then, ads can be run every other week or for two weeks out of three. This is called "flight buying." An on/off schedule can leave the impression that you're advertising for a long period while you may only be paying for half the time.

"Hammock buying" is another possibility. With this strategy, the campaign buys heavily for a week to establish recognition. For the next several weeks, only a sprinkling of ads are purchased to maintain a background image. Then in the final two weeks, extensive use is again made of paid media.

Massachusetts State Senator Patricia McGovern used one very effective technique to build interest in her campaign that ultimately defeated a long-term incumbent. Through a series of newspaper ads designed like a comic strip, she depicted the current senator as an aging ball player who could no longer "deliver" for the home team. In typical cartoon fashion, the strip built suspense with each installment. Then, in the final days before the election, the strip showed a rookie "phenom," Pat McGovern, coming off the bench to save the game.

It may sound corny, but the comic strip made voters pay attention. They remembered Pat McGovern's name as they were reminded of the incumbent's declining abilities. And the baseball metaphor may have subtlely diffused some of the sexual prejudice against the female challenger.

Services and Fees

Three different types of costs are associated with the use of paid media specialists: creative fees; production expenses; and time/ space buying charges. Each of these services may be purchased separately, but often advertising agencies will try to sell packages to your campaign.

Creative fees are what you pay someone to write or design a broadcast spot, newspaper ad, campaign sign, or direct mail solicitation. These are all one-time charges, that are billed at a rate negotiated when the work is accepted. The creative process is the most critical part of paid media. The assistance of a professional is mandatory, either on a fee-for-service or pro bono basis.

Production expenses include charges for recording an advertising spot, laying out and printing a leaflet, or setting type. Professional services are helpful in these areas, but skilled volunteers can do much of the work if the creative design is clear. There is great variation in the charges by different shops. Get several bids for the paid portion before you make any decisions.

Time/space buying charges apply to newspapers, radio, television, and billboards. When professionals buy time or space, the publication or broadcast station pays them 15 percent of the total billing as a commission. A campaign placing the ad directly generally has to pay the full price. Therefore, it is nearly always beneficial to use a professional time/space buyer to do the job.

In the advertising business, the 15 percent commission usually covers creative fees as well as time/space buying charges. If you use a specialist only for the latter function, the campaign should be able to bargain to have a portion of the commission refunded or applied to the purchase of additional ads. A volunteer time/space buyer may be willing to return the entire 15 percent to the campaign—that can really extend the paid media budget.

A professional time/space buyer is also valuable for non economic reasons. Purchasing airtime or ad space involves more than meshing the media survey and the demographics in the Nielsen and Arbitron books with the campaign's target population. Advertising costs and placement are both negotiable. Although a station might list a firm price for a spot, they'll probably be willing to charge less if the time is still unsold one week before airtime. A local professional usually has the contacts required to make the best deals as well as the knowledge to identify the most effective placements for your ads.

Direct Mail

As a fundraising device with an audience already known to be sympathetic, direct mail can be productive. Voter persuasion mail can also be used to reach members of a specialized constituency with a letter designed around their particular concerns. With a computer, you can even personalize the letters with individual salutations. You can, for example, send a letter about senior citizens' issues to every registered voter over the age of sixty-five. But you won't be able to get their feedback, as you could if you contacted them in person

To make your direct mail most effective, no matter what your purpose, use an experienced copywriter and designer. Unless your mailing grips the recipient's attention, it will be thrown out unopened. Often, printing a teaser line like "Help Clean Up the Mess at the State House" on the front of the envelope will do the trick. Have addresses typed individually, either by hand or computer, and use postage stamps instead of a printed bulk permit so you avoid the look of a machine labeled mass mailing.

Once the envelope is opened, you still have to keep the voter interested. Use a bright color ink for the letterhead. Put your strongest message into the first paragraph and keep your arguments to a minimum. It's best to make only one key point per letter.

Though some skilled direct mail specialists have success with multipage mailings, we believe most local campaigns should limit their letters to one page. It's easier to write and edit a short piece, and it's more likely that the voter will read it to the end. Ask for something specific in the letter, whether a contribution, volunteer time, or a vote. And remember to thank the reader for his or her help. A postscript after the candidate's signature has been a proven technique in directing readers' eyes down the page.

Include a response form with every mailing. In this way your voter persuasion efforts can also be used to recruit volunteers and raise money. Your best bet is to include a fundraising return envelope that the campaign has printed in bulk for multiple purposes. A sample return envelope is illustrated on page 183.

Don't overstuff the envelope. A letter, a leaflet, and a response form are sufficient. Be prepared to send more information to anybody who requests it, but keep your direct mail simple.

Finally, remember that your direct mail will only be as good as the lists you use. Make sure the names you select are appropriate for the message you want to deliver and that addresses are up to date. Direct mail is costly enough without wasting money on printing and postage that ends up at the dead letter office.

Leaflets

Leaflets are much cheaper than direct mail, with printing costs of only a couple of pennies apiece; however, they also present significant drawbacks. Not only is their message one-directional, but they are extremely impersonal. Unlike direct mail, there's no way to make a leaflet appear to have come directly from the candidate. As a result, many of your leaflets will be thrown away without being read, especially in neighborhoods that have already been saturated by other candidates.

Again, the help of experienced copywriters, designers, and printers, whether paid professionals or campaign volunteers, is critical. Reproducing an unproofed, long-winded text on a fuzzy mimeograph machine will defeat whatever the leaflet may try to accomplish.

When in doubt about leaflet design, keep it simple! Too many candidates fall into the trap of: "I paid for this piece of paper, and I'm going to print on every square inch of it." Prune out tangential messages and unnecessary words. Most voters have neither the time nor the interest to wade through hundreds of lines of copy. You can't afford to have them miss your message because it is hidden in the middle of a lengthy text.

Don't be shy about looking at literature from previous races for design ideas. A concept that worked before might work again and be adaptable to your campaign. In any case, start with a dramatic headline because people decide whether to read a leaflet at first glance. Use a photograph or drawing as another attention-getting device. Set the leaflet text in type larger than most newspapers or magazines use to make it easy to read. And allow lots of white space in your layout to frame your message.

In the early stages of the campaign when you are primarily building name recognition, leaflets with the candidate's name and basic campaign theme printed in large letters are often sufficient. Leaflets that will be posted on bulletin boards or outside locations should be limited to one side of a single piece of paper. Multipage layouts can be used for basic candidate brochures, but the longer the leaflet, the more important the design. Work closely with your artists and printers to make sure all your leaflets deliver your message cost-effectively.

Campaign Paraphernalia

Almost from the moment you announce your candidacy, your mailbox will begin filling with offers to sell you political advertising materials ranging from bumper stickers, buttons, and lawn signs to balloons, nail files, and pocket calendars. Though these gimmicks are often a favorite of campaign volunteers and collectors, there's little evidence that they perform any useful role beyond promoting your candidate's name.

Even that application should be considered critically. The cost for these materials can quickly add up. Too often, low-budget campaigns invest in these products simply because "all the other candidates have bumper stickers." Whenever you are tempted to make such a purchase, think carefully about how they will help fulfill your basic mission: repetitive, persuasive communication with likely supporters. Make sure you are using your limited resources most intelligently.

Remember, name recognition is their primary purpose. That means the candidate's name should dominate any materials. If there's additional space, add a few words that reinforce your campaign theme. Keep the message consistent with other communications. For example, if your candidate's major focus is crime control, have buttons, bumper stickers, and lawn signs say something like "Donnelly: For Safer Streets."

Be sure to keep your target audience in mind, both when you produce and when you distribute campaign paraphernalia. For example, there's no point in wasting materials on people who are not likely to vote. Nor does it make much sense to give away nail files displaying your name at the local men's club.

Timing is also very important. If you've decided to post lawn signs, consider whether you want volunteers to set them all out on the same night for greatest impact, or show building momentum by putting them up over several weeks.

Buy quality products if you decide to use any paraphernalia. You'll lose credibility as well as supporters if your buttons fall apart or the printing on your bumper stickers and lawn signs fades away before Election Day.

Maintaining Political Control

Professionals ensure the most cost-effective use of your paid media budget, but advertising specialists are translators, not experts in election strategy.

Political control should always remain in the hands of the campaign leadership. Advertising professionals must be made to understand that their work is just one part of your overall strategy, which defined your message and target audience. They should never be allowed to function independently.

It is particularly important that the work of advertising specialists be meshed with the field and press operations, since these are the other ways your campaign message is delivered to large numbers of persuadable voters. Theme and timing must be consistent. Coordination is the role of the campaign manager and, ultimately, the candidate. Any proposal from a specialist that is inconsistent with your political judgment should be rejected. After all, it's your campaign, not an advertising agency's.

8

FUNDRAISING

SOME CANDIDATES CAN SKIP THIS CHAPTER.
YOU PROBABLY CAN'T.

The candidate who is independently wealthy doesn't have to worry about fundraising. Neither does the candidate who is the darling of a special interest with deep pockets. But if you don't fall into either category read on.

As long as political campaigns are privately financed, raising money is a necessary step on your way to victory. It's a myth that a highly motivated volunteer campaign can be run without funds. However carefully you budget, you will still need enough money to support the activities to make persuasive contacts with voters.

Money is *not*, however, the magic ingredient for campaigns. No matter how much you raise it won't take the place of a clear strategy, a good plan to communicate a repetitive, persuasive message to voters, and hard work.

The greatest obstacle you'll have to overcome is the notion that fundraising is difficult and everyone hates to do it. The fact is that billions of dollars are raised every year for campaigns, charities, issues, and community organizations. Obviously, there are millions of people who regularly give to causes and candidates they support. And there are thousands of others with experience in raising funds. The trick is to find those people and involve them in your campaign.

The Fundraising Team

Finance Coordinator

First you'll need a finance coordinator. Though responsibility for certain events can be delegated to others, the finance coordinator must be a good manager able to oversee the entire fundraising effort. The candidate must have confidence in the person chosen for this important role because the finance coordinator will be the campaign's direct representative to donors. The finance coordinator should also be well-respected in the community and capable of motivating others.

There should be a clear delineation of responsibilities between the finance coordinator and the campaign treasurer, which is covered in Chapter 3. In general, the finance coordinator oversees raising funds and the treasurer oversees spending them. In addition to paying the bills and keeping the financial records, the treasurer usually collects and deposits all contributions. The important thing is to work out a system for handling funds that meets your accounting and reporting requirements and also keeps the finance coordinator informed of all fundraising receipts on a regular basis.

The finance coordinator's early estimates of how much money can be raised during the course of the campaign are an important foundation for developing the budgets discussed earlier. For this reason, it is important for this person to work closely with the campaign manager to revise those estimates if necessary. The success of the fundraising effort is the major factor that necessitates budget changes during a campaign. It is important for the campaign manager to be informed not only of dollars raised, but also of the fundraising projections on a weekly basis.

If you can recruit someone who has done political fundraising before, you'll be one step ahead of the game. These people are likely to have lists of political donors or access to them. But don't use past campaign experience as your only measure. If an individual is highly motivated to raise money for the candidate, a wide variety of community and occupational skills can be translated to campaign fundraising. Consider, for example, someone who has raised funds for a neighborhood group, the YWCA, or other charitable organizations.

Finance Committee

Setting up a Finance Committee is a good way to give key people a role in the fundraising effort. Members assist the coordinator by identifying donors, soliciting contributions for the candidate, and often hosting fundraising events. The best approach is to make the Finance Committee representative of your entire district. This way the campaign will have contacts with the broadest range of potential donors, including various ethnic, racial, and religious groups. Select members from all the district's geographic areas and individuals from key occupation groups as well.

A diverse Finance Committee guarantees that donors who don't know the candidate can be approached by a campaign supporter who is an acquaintance, colleague, or member of their peer group. It also helps with fundraising efforts targeted at specific groups—a union representative can contact union members, a lawyer can contact other lawyers.

Schedule periodic meetings with the candidate to update the Finance Committee members on the campaign's progress and to let them know how vital their efforts are to its success. Create an atmosphere of friendly competition to encourage committee members to meet the campaign's fundraising goals.

The Candidate

The finance coordinator, the Finance Committee, and volunteers all play an important role in fundraising, but the central figure is the candidate. Every prospective candidate should heed the warning: "If you can't personally ask for contributions to your campaign, don't run."

If you find asking for money difficult, put the request in perspective. Remember, you are already asking for something of value. You are asking countless numbers of people to give long hours of their time as staff and volunteers, and many more to give you the confidence of their vote for public office. You may not grow to love fundraising, but with practice you can develop a smooth technique to ask for financial support. The key is believing in yourself and your campaign.

The best practice is to begin with family and close friends. They are not only your best source of early money, but offer a friendly audience for developing a fundraising approach that works for you. Don't be hesitant. Donald Page Moore, a fundraiser for Bernard Weisberg's Independent campaign for the Illinois Constitutional Convention put it this way in *Winning Elections:* "If you're not afraid of losing friends, go to everybody you know—tackle them in the hall, phone them, write them a letter and then call them and simply say, 'Give me money.' "

Planning the Fundraising Program

However large or small your budget, fundraising is too important to be left to ad hoc efforts. Soliciting contributions requires careful planning. Not only must an adequate amount of money be raised, but projected income must also meet the campaign's cash flow requirements.

Typically, campaigns find it much easier to raise money close to the election, when voter interest is high, than early on. But fundraising should begin as soon as the decision to run is made. Money raised early in the campaign has several advantages:

• It allows you to plan more accurately. If you know the money is in the bank, you can make commitments for things that require advance payment, such as printing and radio time.

• The credibility of your campaign increases in the eyes of potential donors if you demonstrate the ability to raise money early in the race. This image can be an important one, especially for a challenger. Early fundraising success may even help keep possible opponents out of the race.

• Building up a donor list early in the campaign gives you ample time to resolicit them for additional contributions.

The program and the cash flow budgets you've prepared tell how much money you need and when you need it. Now you must draw up a fundraising plan to meet these deadlines. A week-by-week plan should describe in detail what activities will be conducted and estimate the net income from each.

In designing the fundraising plan, you should include a combination of activities designed for three general categories of potential donors:

• Small donor: Under $25

- Medium donor: $25-$100

- Large donor: $100 and over

These categories are usually based on the size of a single contribution, rather than the donor's total contributions over the course of the campaign. This is because the characteristics of a donor who writes $15 checks (even if they write three of them throughout the campaign) differ from a donor who writes a $50 check. You want to design your fundraising activities to approach each donor at the appropriate level, and through resolicitation maximize their contribution total.

Methods of solicitation and the types of events you plan will vary depending on the category, but all potential donors should be made to feel that they can play a part in the campaign. The broader your fundraising base the better.

Identifying Donor Prospects

The finance coordinator should begin to identify potential donors immediately. Put the names of targeted medium and large donors on a file card with their names and addresses, phone numbers, and the level of donation that can be expected. Also note the source of the name, particularly if it came from a supporter who might be helpful in requesting a contribution. These same cards can be used to keep a record of the contacts made and contributions received from each donor. File them alphabetically and they'll be easy to find and update.

How do you build a file of potential donors? Start with the candidate's friends, family, and professional associates. Include everyone the candidate has contributed to or worked for in previous campaigns. These political colleagues are a source of support as well as a source of names of large major donors from whom funds can also be solicited.

Contribution lists from previous campaigns whose constituency and message were similar to yours are another good source of names. The giving history these lists provide also helps you solicit donors for contributions at the appropriate level. These lists can be obtained from past candidates who are not running for re-election (or their finance coordinator) and from contributor lists filed according to your state's campaign disclosure laws. If you're

SAMPLE DONOR PROSPECT CARD

Contact Person: _____

Name _____

Mailing Address _____

_____

Business Phone _____

Home Phone _____

Source of Name: _____

Previous Giving History: _____

_____

_____

Print on reverse side of card:

	Contact Date	By	Response	Amount Contributed	Thank You
1.					
2.					
3.					
4.					
5.					

running in a general election you may get some lists from your political party.

Look for other prospects among the members of groups to which the candidate belongs or that support the campaign's priority issues. You may also find support among groups that strongly oppose your opponent's positions. Requests for membership or contributor lists from these organizations should be coordinated with the campaign's efforts to secure their endorsement and recruit volunteers.

The plan should show how you will use the various fundraising methods, including:

• Personal solicitation

- Direct mail

- Resolicitation of previous donors

- Fundraising events

- Moneymaking activities

- Group and political action committee contributions

These methods are universal. Each one is described in detail in the following section. You need only creatively adapt them to your particular campaign.

The possibilities are endless. If you encourage volunteer involvement in the fundraising effort, you will find that many people will come up with good ideas and then take responsibility for their implementation. The finance coordinator should schedule and supervise these activities to see that the theme is consistent with your overall strategy and that campaign finance laws are followed.

Thank-Yous

Before we go through methods of raising funds, a word about what to do after you raise them. An ironclad rule that you ignore at your own peril: *Every contribution, regardless of the amount, should be acknowledged immediately by a thank-you letter signed by the candidate.*

The more personal the letter, the better. If you have access to a word processor or personal computer and printer, you can send a form letter that includes the contributor's address and a personal salutation. An especially large contribution deserves an even more individualized letter, with some personal details. For example, the letter from the candidate might begin like the sample paragraph on page 167.

If you use a form letter, be sure to change versions periodically to reflect the stages of the campaign. For example, an early letter might say, "Your contribution helped me to launch my campaign . . ."; a later one can refer to the "home stretch" and review some of the campaign's accomplishments.

The importance of this aspect of fundraising cannot be overstated. Thanking people isn't just courtesy, it's an investment in

> Dear (name),
>
> I was very pleased when (name of Finance Committee member who solicited the contribution) told me of your very generous contribution to my campaign. Your solid support and that of other members of (organization) has made it possible for us to move closer to victory on November 6.
>
> Sincerely,
>
> (candidate's signature)

future fundraising. If contributors are convinced their support is really appreciated, you can go back and ask for more. That means not only resoliciting donors prior to Election Day, but building a donor base for future campaigns as well.

Establish a foolproof system for making sure donors receive a thank-you appropriate to the size of their contribution. Acknowledging donors should be one person's responsibility, perhaps an assistant to the finance coordinator. Dividing that responsibility among a number of volunteers opens the possibility that an acknowledgment will be overlooked and a repeat gift lost.

Personal Solicitation

The same principle holds true in fundraising as in voter persuasion activities: the more personal the contact the more effective it will be. For this reason, personal solicitation is by far the most successful form of fundraising. In most campaigns, all early fundraising is done this way.

Because time is so valuable once the campaign heats up, one-on-one solicitation by the candidate is most often restricted to potential donors who can make a substantial contribution to the campaign. A general definition of a large donation is over $100, but this category should be adjusted to whatever is appropriate to your community and the budget for your race. A large donation is one that is worth the investment of the candidate's time for a personal meeting.

The following step-by-step guide for individual fundraising meetings is designed for the candidate, but it can be adpated for any personal solicitations:

• Schedule a meeting with a potential donor. Make it clear that you are going to ask for financial help. If the candidate does not know the donor it is best if the introduction is made by a supporter whom the potential contributor knows and respects. This can be by a prior phone call or by the supporter accompanying the candidate to the fundraising meeting.

• Explain why you need financial support. Bring copies of the campaign plan and budget as back-up resources. Many large donors want to see financial projections before they will write a check.

• Mention other respected individuals and organizations who have contributed.

• Suggest a specific amount for a contribution. Your Donor Prospect Card can be helpful in determining the amount to request. Ask for somewhat more than you expect to get. If your request is too high, you will flatter donors by overestimating their resources. On the other hand, you may get what you ask for.

• Once you have the commitment of a contribution, ask the donor to help you raise additional funds from friends and associates. Don't leave without getting the names of additional people to solicit.

• Remember to thank the donor at the end of the meeting and send a written acknowledgment from the candidate soon thereafter.

You may want to include a "pledge system" in your personal solicitations. In this case, donors are asked to make a commitment to give a certain amount at regular intervals in the campaign. This method can sometimes increase an individual's total contribution. But because early money is so valuable and a pledge system requires staff time for follow-up, always try first for the single large contribution.

If a Finance Committee is established, the number of people who can personally solicit large and medium donors is greatly expanded. Working with the finance coordinator, committee members should compile a list of prospective donors. These prospects should be grouped by their probable level of giving. Then divide the list, with each member taking responsibility for contacting those donors with whom they have a relationship.

Set up a system to keep close track of the assignments that are made. It may be necessary to make adjustments if a Finance Committee member does not follow through. You must be diplomatic, but it's better to reassign a fundraising contact or make it yourself than risk losing a contribution.

Before speaking to prospective donors, committee members should be fully briefed. The task will be easier if they have sufficient information about the candidate, the campaign, and the fundraising drive. The following material is helpful:

- A sample script that highlights the points to be made in the fundraising pitch.

- A summary of the campaign plan and budget. Often you can use the budget to show a donor specifically what the contribution will buy for the campaign: a radio spot, 10,000 leaflets, etc. They can see how their gift has a definite effect on the campaign.

- The candidate's biography and positions on certain key issues, particularly those of interest to the donor. These can be in draft form if campaign literature has not yet been produced.

- Specific instructions on how checks should be made out and an outline of the legal regulations concerning political contributions in your district, as well as your campaign's specific policies.

Role playing fundraising visits at a Finance Committee meeting may help make the process less intimidating. Take turns role playing different kinds of personal and phone solicitation situations. Allow time to answer any questions.

The finance coordinator should contact committee members regularly to check on their progress. It's important to monitor each member's performance so you can change assignments or revise your fundraising projections if necessary. If your committee is large you will find it helpful to use a form similar to the one on page 170 for periodic progress reports.

Contributions at all levels can be personally solicited by everyone involved in the campaign. All campaign supporters should be urged to request contributions from their friends and close associates.

FINANCE COMMITTEE REPORT

Member's Name _____

Telephone #(s) _____

Date of Report: _____

Person Contacted	Date	Result Contribution/Pledge	Comments
1.			
2.			
3.			
4.			
5.			
6.			
7.			
8.			
9.			
10.			

Too often fundraising is treated as a function entirely separate from the rest of the campaign. Many campaign workers assume that the finance coordinator and Finance Committtee members raise the money while everyone else spends it. In fact, everyone involved in the campaign should think of themselves as a fundraiser. This should start with staff and volunteers making a personal contribution. Some campaigns even develop a monthly pledge system to encourage volunteers to contribute. Once they have given, volunteers find it easier to ask their friends to donate.

One candidate for the state legislature in Iowa used a "pyramiding pledge system" as the foundation of her fundraising plan. Each new volunteer signed a pledge card similar to: "To help elect

170

Kathy Baker in the 7th District, I promise to get seven people to give $7 each or seven hours of work to the campaign. . . .'' As the numbers grew, the contributions not only filled the campaign coffers, but also provided good copy for press stories about the candidate who stressed her reliance on grass-roots support. The ''Lucky 7'' stories greatly aided the candidate's name recognition and her volunteer corps—ranging, as the press said, ''from teenagers to their grandmothers''—grew to over 300 by Election Day.

Direct Mail

Before we extol the virtues of direct mail for campaign fundraising, a word about its limitations. Direct mail is expensive, requires a great deal of lead time, is less effective than personal appeals, and is only as good as the lists you are using. By all means include a fundraising pitch in all of the mail your field organization has planned, that way your communication serves two purposes: delivering the campaign's message to potential voters, and raising money. But if your budget is small, think twice before embarking on a specific direct mail effort to test lists of potential contributors. Even the experts consider a 2 percent rate of response to be good when you are using cold lists. Remember, both printers and the post office require payment in advance. Bulk-rate permits also must be reserved and purchased in advance, so decide early enough to allow the necessary time in your printing schedule.

The most effective use of direct mail is to resolicit your own donors (which is covered in depth in the next section). That's because the single most important factor in the success of direct mail fundraising is the list you use. There's no better list than your own proven contributors, either from earlier in the campaign or from previous elections.

To develop other lists for direct mail fundraising appeals, look to sources similar to those used for personal solicitation. The best names are those people who are likely to support your candidate and who also have a history of making campaign contributions. Whether the amounts are large or small, the people most likely to give are those who have given before.

If you are doing a large mailing (over 500 pieces) pretest your list to determine whether the return you receive will be worth the expense. To do this choose between 10 and 20 percent of the total number of names (not less than a hundred) at random to receive the mailing. If you are testing more than one list, be sure to code the reply card so you can determine the number of responses and the size of the contributions derived from each list.

You should receive the bulk of the responses within ten days after your letter is delivered. Allow approximately three weeks for all returns and calculate whether the result was positive (a net gain), a break-even, or a loss. Even a break-even result may be positive in the long run because you will have generated names that can be resolicited for a second contribution later in the campaign.

There are two schools of thought about the length of fundraising letters. The first traces its origins to Morris Dees's fundraising appeals for George McGovern's 1972 presidential campaign. Those extraordinarily successful letters averaged five pages in length! The other school believes voters don't read beyond the first page and makes short and persuasive arguments in less than one and a half pages. For state and local campaigns, few of which involve issues as complex as in a presidential election, we think short is better.

As a rule, letters with individualized names, addresses, and salutations get a higher rate of response than standard "Dear Friend" letters. But, of course, personalized letters are more time consuming and costly to produce, so you must make trade-offs. At any rate, target the appeal to the specific audience you are trying to reach. For example, you may prepare several letters, one for each constituency or group on your lists. The major themes will be consistent, but you can emphasize your position (or record) on an issue of concern to each group. These letters can be signed by the candidate, the finance coordinator, or by a supporter who is a well-known member of the particular group. For example, the local teachers' union president who is an active supporter could sign a letter addressed to other educators.

Always include a return envelope in fundraising mailings. One issue to consider is whether the return envelope should include prepaid postage. There is some evidence that it increases the rate of return, but given the expense it may well be a luxury you cannot afford.

If you have the volunteer resources, consider setting up a phone bank to do follow-up calls shortly after the direct mail is delivered. The personal follow-up will greatly increase your rate of return.

Resolicitation of Previous Donors

People who have given money to the candidate have a stake in the campaign. Especially if they were promptly thanked and assured their support made a difference, they are very likely to make a second contribution to ensure victory.

Every benchmark in a campaign presents an opportunity for resoliciting donors. If you are launching your radio spots, you can ask people for additional contributions to pay for them. If your opponent is launching a media blitz, you can ask for money to counter it. If you receive an important endorsement, ask for money to exploit this expression of support. If your opponent gets the endorsement, ask for money to counter the power of the ''political establishment.''

Ideally, you should ask for repeat contributions in the same way you solicited the first contribution. This is not always possible, however, and not always necessary. A large donor who was solicited the first time in person might be solicited a second time with a personal phone call from the candidate or the person who solicited the first gift. A large donor may even respond to a personal letter, but if you write letters to large donors, follow up with phone calls to those who don't respond.

Medium and small donors should also receive regular solicitation letters asking for additional money. Resolicitation is such an important part of any campaign fundraising effort, we've included a sample letter and a basic outline to adapt to your own campaign:

• Tell the donor that the contribution has helped. List briefly what you have accomplished because of the support.

• Before you get halfway down the first page, say that you need more money.

• Tie your request to some specific event or opportunity, such as the opening of a campaign office, a major literature drop, or media buys.

• Ask for a specific contribution or range of contributions. Never suggest they give you less than the last time. Always try to increase the gift. Versions of form letters that state different amounts for different categories of donors are an effective way of doing this.

• Impose a deadline even if you have to invent it. Donors are most receptive when they are first contacted. Don't let them put the letter aside to consider later. Say you must have the money within ten days or you'll miss an important deadline. Or claim you're having a strategy meeting on the eighteenth and must know what funds are available for the final media buys. Set your deadline ten days from the day the prospect receives the letter.

• Thank the donor again, and remind him or her that an additional contribution will make a decisive difference in your election.

SAMPLE RESOLICITATION LETTER

★ Susan
Richards
for
Senator

Dear (name)

Your contribution to the Susan Richards for State Senate campaign has worked a miracle!

With your financial support and the enthusiastic efforts of hundreds of dedicated volunteers, Susan has been transformed from a "dark horse" to a front-runner in this important election.

Press coverage has grown substantially with this new credibility and we have recently gained the endorsements of leaders of organizations like (give examples)

To make the most of these endorsements we need your help once again.

We are planning to publicize these endorsements with carefully targeted mailings to voters in the 5th Senatorial District. Volunteers are standing by to get this mailing out, but cash is very short.

Your contribution of $25 will pay for printing and postage for (number) of these crucial letters; $50 will help us reach (number) voters.

We must give the printer a firm order on the eighteenth of this month. We must receive your contribution by that date so we can determine how many uncommitted voters we can reach. Every vote counts and we urgently need your help.

Won't you help us continue to build momentum by writing a check today? Your past support has brought us a long way. Your continuing support can put Susan Richards in the State Senate.

Sincerely,

P.S. Remember, we must make critical decisions by the eighteenth of this month. Please mail your check as soon as possible.

Fundraising Events

Fundraising events can be planned for either large, medium, or small donors. The admission fee should be appropriate to the level of the contribution those you plan to invite can make. To decide on a ticket price, consider how many tickets you must sell at different prices to meet your fundraising goal. Remember to consider your costs, such as a catered dinner at a hotel or Kentucky Fried Chicken for a picnic, before projecting your likely profit from ticket sales. For example:

Ticket Price	Event Cost Per Ticket	Profit Per Ticket	Ticket Sales Required to Net $3,000
$100	$15	$85	36
50	8	42	72
25	5	20	150
5	0	5	600

You can also design a single event that includes all levels of donors. One way to do this is to ask people to contribute variable amounts. For example, the invitation may list different contribution levels for "patrons," "sponsors," or "friends." Often, these people are listed by name under these headings in the program for the event. Or you can plan a small high-donor event, such as a cocktail party or dinner, to precede or follow a larger medium- or small-donor event. The high-dollar donors will get to spend more time with the candidate, or with a featured guest, for their extra contribution.

The larger the event, the more important it is to delegate organizing responsibility to an experienced event coordinator. The major tasks include arrangements for the event itself and supervision of ticket sales or invitations. These jobs can be split between two volunteers. Handling the logistics for a smoothly run event takes different skills than motivating a cadre of ticket sellers. One of the two may be responsible for overall supervision of the event, or both may report directly to the finance coordinator. Any plans for media coverage of the event should be coordinated with the press secretary.

Always try to keep your expenses as low as possible to increase your profit from the event. Check carefully to see which costs you might normally incur could be contributed. For example, holding the gathering at someone's home can save the cost of renting a hall. If possible, have volunteers prepare the food instead of catering and get someone else to contribute the entertainment. However, be careful to comply with your local campaign finance laws for recording and reporting in-kind contributions.

Now comes the toughest part of the operation: ticket sales. Small donor events require especially careful planning and organization since you must sell a large number of tickets to raise a significant amount of money. It's usually easiest to handle these events with both prepaid tickets and a pay-at-the-door option. Adding a dollar to the price of tickets bought on the day of the event will encourage people to pay in advance. This helps to estimate attendance and also reduces log jams at the door.

There are two basic sales techniques: person-to-person, supporters selling tickets to others directly, and mailed invitations followed up by phone calls. If you have motivated volunteers, person-to-person sales are the fastest, least expensive, and most reliable method. Start with the sponsors of the event. In addition to making a contribution, ask each of them to sell a certain number of tickets. Recruit the candidate's family, friends, and volunteers to be ticket sellers as well.

Set up a good recordkeeping system, noting the seller's name and phone number, the quantity of tickets taken (and the numbers if they are in sequence), and the date. Prepare a simple packet for each seller with the tickets and an information sheet about the event. Put the deadline for selling tickets in bold letters. Tell how checks should be made out and to whom and where the money should be turned in.

Let each ticket seller know that their efforts are the key to the success of the event, and that you will be checking with them regularly for progress reports. Then, do exactly that. Persistent follow-up phone calls will then turn the seller's commitment into dollars.

Invitations sent by mail require more expense and more lead time. As a general rule, invitations should be mailed three to four weeks before the event, which means you have to design and print the invitation, gather lists, and schedule volunteers for addressing envelopes well in advance of the date.

The best way to assure the success of a fundraising event is to ask key supporters to become event sponsors. Each sponsor donates a certain amount of money in advance and allows the use of his or her name on the invitation. It may be a small list: "Helen Jones, Stewart Moore, and Barbara Taylor invite you to meet (candidate) for the City Council at a Cocktail Party at the home of . . ."

Or it may be a whole column of sponsors listed inside the invitation. In any case, you get double benefit: the list of recognizable names encourages the invitee to join the sponsors at the event, while at the same time it reduces the campaign's risk by covering the expenses and perhaps even showing a profit before the first ticket is sold.

It is helpful to have supporters personally address invitations to their friends and include a handwritten note urging them to attend. However, printed invitations alone are not sufficient to ensure a capacity crowd. Dividing the list of invitees among volunteers for follow-up phone calls will significantly increase attendance. A concentrated telephone follow-up, using a written script, should begin seven to ten days before the event. If invitees cannot attend, they should be encouraged to send a contribution anyway. Have the volunteers record the results of their phone calls and check on their progress regularly. A large part of your financial success will depend on this personal follow-up.

Enclosing a reply card and return envelope with the invitation generally increases your rate of response. It not only makes it easier for invitees to respond, it also gives them an opportunity to express interest or support if they are not able to attend. Each reply card should allow for the following information:

☐ "I'm unable to attend, but I'm enclosing a contribution."
☐ "I'll volunteer to help in the campaign. Please have someone contact me."
☐ "Please send me information about (the candidate's) position on _____."

If the program you have planned is enough of a draw, you may be able to attract an audience broader than just potential supporters and contributors. Such events often center around a celebrity people want to meet. Another possibility is benefit concerts. These can range from a string quartet in a private home to a west-

SAMPLE REPLY CARD

RSVP to: Friends of Diane Walters
152 Main St.
Gary, Indiana
(219) 555-0123

_____ I will be happy to attend the event and to meet Diane Walters. My personal contribution to her campaign is enclosed.

_____ I cannot attend but I want to help elect a progressive woman to the State Senate. I enclose a contribution for Diane's campaign in the amount of $ _____ .

_____ I want to volunteer to help Diane get elected. Please have someone contact me.

_____ I'm interested in Diane's campaign. Please send me information about her position on _____ .

Checks should be made payable to: Walters for Senate

Paid for by the Diane Walters for State Senate Committee

ern band at an outdoor barbecue. Building a crowd for these types of public events usually involves substantial advertising—such as distributing leaflets or posting signs in stores—and less reliance on personal invitations.

Ten for Ten

The pyramiding technique is another good way to involve volunteers in putting on fundraising events where small contributions quickly add up. The following Ten for Ten program has been used as a successful Republican fundraiser around the country. Use it as a model to develop your own variation.

To begin, select ten members of a Ten for Ten Committee (or Ten for Your Candidate). Each member is asked to recruit ten people to give Ten for Ten parties. Your goal: a hundred hosts and hostesses, each of whom will invite ten guests. Each invitee (or couple, family, etc.) is asked to contribute $10. At 1,000 guests times $10 each, that's $10,000 in campaign contributions.

The parties can be held over a period of several weeks, or all in one week, as your campaign calendar dictates. Remember, you don't want to take volunteers' time too close to a big canvassing drive or other important event.

The individual hosting each party contributes the food and refreshments and provides the entertainment. Party themes can be as varied as dinner by a gourmet cook, a backyard picnic, cards and games, or an evening of old movies played on a video recorder. If enough people in your district have cable television service, you might consider scheduling the parties for the night the candidate appears on a special cable TV program.

You'll need good organization to pull this off, but it can be done with one coordinator and a highly motivated committee. It takes only nine easy steps:

1. Recruit the members of the Ten for Ten Committee.

2. Committee members contact friends, relatives, neighbors, etc. to recruit ten individuals to give parties.

3. Names are given to the coordinator and thank-you letters are sent to each host/hostess.

4. Starter kits are sent to each individual hosting a party; they contain invitations with blank spaces for the host's name, time, date, and place; party suggestions; and instructions. Include the committee member's name and telephone number to contact if they need assistance.

5. Each host/hostess is called by the member of the Ten for Ten Committee who recruited them to be sure they received their starter kit and to answer any questions.

6. One week before the party the individual giving the party is sent a party kit containing campaign brochures, contribution envelopes, receipts, and instructions on how checks should be made out or cash contributions recorded.

7. Three days before the party, committee members check with each of their hosts/hostesses to be certain they received the party kit. Hand-deliver extra sets of materials that may have been lost in transit.

8. The day after the party collect the report from each host/hostess with the names and addresses of guests and their contributions.

9. Finally, send thank-you letters signed by the candidate to each host and hostess.

Visibility at Fundraising Events

The primary purpose of a fundraising event is to raise money, but the larger the event, the greater the opportunities for voter persuasion and volunteer recruitment. At any large event, there will be undecided voters who have been brought along as guests, supporters who can become volunteers, and volunteers who need some encouragement and inspiration. The program of the event should give the candidate good exposure and convey the enthusiasm of the campaign.

Moneymaking Activities

Most fundraising events are aimed at people who want to support the candiate. A "money-maker" is a special type of fundraising event; it can be a way for volunteers to earn money for the campaign from people who may not have any commitment to the candidate.

A bake sale to benefit the campaign is a typical money-maker. Yard sales, raffles, or bingo games (where allowed by law) are other possibilities.

Such moneymaking activities have not been limited to state and local campaigns. A former congressional aide tapped his Washington, D.C., friends for their secondhand junk when he successfully challenged an incumbent in 1974. The event was so successful that Representative Phil Sharpe of Indiana repeated the yard sale every two years, raising $1,000 to $3,000 for his reelection campaign. The secret is to have volunteers go out and collect the items that people pledge to donate. Don't wait for them to bring it in.

One big advantage of these techniques is that they can raise campaign funds without any investment of the candidate's time. The amounts of money may be small, but such events generate cash from the resource many campaigns have in greatest supply: volunteer time.

Money-makers can be run with less organization and lower overhead costs than fundraising events. They also provide a good way for teenagers to become involved in the campaign. Everyone has some experience with glee club car washes, PTA bake sales, and the like. Create ways to turn that experience into money for the campaign.

The first goal is to make money, but don't overlook any opportunity for gaining increased recognition for the candidate. Always have posters, campaign literature, and pledge cards on hand. The visibility may provide good publicity and attract more volunteers and contributions.

One candidate with a strong environmental record in the Vermont legislature earns both money and campaign publicity by collecting returnable bottles and cans. Since her political career began as an advocate for the state's "bottle bill," collecting bottles and cans reinforces her campaign theme. Similarly, if your campaign theme stresses community involvement in a grass-roots campaign, local newspapers might be happy to fill some space with a picture (provided by you) of neighborhood people getting out to work for their candidate.

Group and Political Action Committee Contributions

Political action committees (PACs) are a rapidly growing feature of American politics. Their growing influence is most clearly measured in congressional and U.S. senatorial campaigns where the Federal Elections Commission reports that PAC contributions in 1984 exceeded $100 million.

But PACs play a role at the state level as well. In Massachusetts alone, there are more than 200 registered political action committees that contribute to state legislative and mayoral elections.

To be sure, the overwhelming majority of all PAC contributions go to the incumbent officeholder. Start with that as a given and then consider if PACs are a potential fundraising resource for your campaign. It is also best to consider at the outset whether the PAC contributions received by you, or by your opponent, will be a political issue in the campaign.

Compile a list of the organizations in your district that make contributions to political candidates. The secretary of state may maintain a complete list of registered committees. You can also review the financial reports of previous campaigns. If you are running in a general election, start with the partisan groups in your district, such as the North End Democratic Club, or the Suburban Republican Women's Club. Next, decide which groups aligned with the issues you advocate might be willing to make a contribution to help elect an ally.

The candidate or campaign manager should make the initial contact. Some groups may require the candidate to fill out a questionnaire on policy positions or attend a membership or board meeting to be interviewed in order to secure the endorsement.

There are also an increasing number of national organizations, such as taxpayer, environmental, and union groups that have recognized the significant impact that state and local offices have on their issues and are making contributions to these races. Many of the nonpartisan national women's organizations support candidates for state offices as a part of their leadership development programs for future congressional races. If you are running a major race, don't overlook these national sources.

Organizations should be contacted early in the campaign. Not only can they provide needed financial assistance, but some may provide in-kind services that can greatly reduce campaign expenses. In addition to a contribution, ask the organization to assist your campaign by recruiting their members as volunteers or sending an endorsement mailing to members in your district.

Including Fundraising Appeals in All Campaign Programs

Maximize your fundraising efforts by integrating financial appeals into all campaign activities. One of the most useful tools to help you do this is a campaign reply envelope that can be sealed and returned to the campaign with a contribution. These are usually flap envelopes like the sample on page 183. These "Yes, I Will Help Elect (Candidate) to the City Council" envelopes can be used to recruit volunteers as well.

The candidate and the campaign aides should always have these envelopes on hand to give to people who express support. At any event where it would be appropriate, the candidate or a supporter should make a pitch for funds and pass out contribution envelopes. Depending on your budget, consider including the reply envelope in all mailings sent by the field organization to potential supporters. Remember, neither volunteers nor contributors will step forward spontaneously. You have to ask.

The door-to-door canvass presents another fundraising opportunity. It is not unusual for the canvass to serve the purpose of voter identification and fundraising at the same time. In addition to the usual canvassing materials, volunteers should carry:

- A receipt book with carbon copies in which the canvasser can record the name and address of the donor and the amount of the contribution; the original receipt should be signed and given to the donor.

SAMPLE CAMPAIGN REPLY ENVELOPE

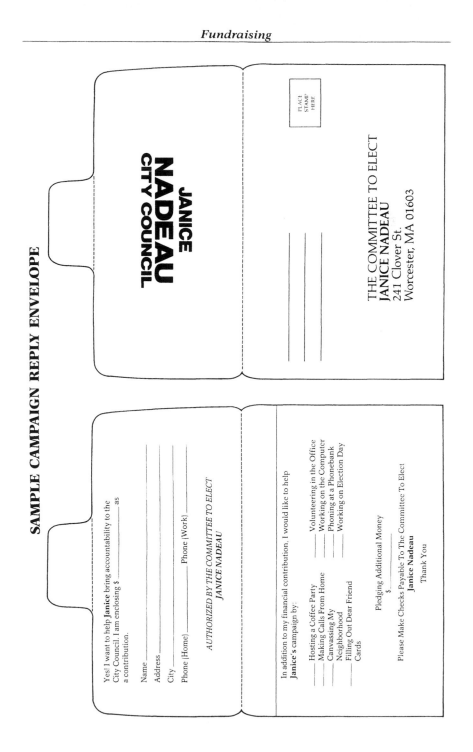

JANICE NADEAU CITY COUNCIL

PLACE STAMP HERE

THE COMMITTEE TO ELECT
JANICE NADEAU
241 Clover St.
Worcester, MA 01603

Yes! I want to help **Janice** bring accountability to the City Council. I am enclosing $_____ as a contribution.

Name _____

Address _____

City _____ Phone (Work) _____

Phone (Home) _____

AUTHORIZED BY THE COMMITTEE TO ELECT
JANICE NADEAU

In addition to my financial contribution, I would like to help **Janice's** campaign by:

_____ Hosting a Coffee Party
_____ Making Calls From Home
_____ Canvassing My Neighborhood
_____ Filling Out Dear Friend Cards
_____ Volunteering in the Office
_____ Working on the Computer
_____ Phoning at a Phonebank
_____ Working on Election Day

_____ Pledging Additional Money
$_____

Please Make Checks Payable To The Committee To Elect
Janice Nadeau

Thank You

183

- Campaign reply envelopes that can be left with voters who are not interested in making an immediate donation.

- Invitations to an upcoming fundraising event.

With these materials, volunteers can follow up when they encounter a strong supporter. They should make it clear to supporters that the candidate needs help to win the race and ask them to volunteer or make a financial contribution to the campaign.

Phone canvassers should be equally well prepared to ask for volunteers and money when they identify a supporter. Here's a case where staff coordination can save time and multiply resources. The finance coordinator and the field coordinator should ensure that fundraising instructions are included in the volunteers' canvassing scripts.

Recordkeeping

Obviously, if you are going to ask donors for additional contributions, you must have good records of who they are, how to contact them, and how much they've already given. You also need to keep accurate records to comply with the finance reporting requirements in your state. These laws should be thoroughly researched at the very beginning of the campaign. Start by contacting the secretary of state's office. This is usually the agency charged with administering state election laws and should be able to provide a copy of campaign finance regulations as well as help you interpret their application to your campaign. The local registrar of voters or town clerk will have the same information for municipal elections. Pay special attention to filing dates and regulations regarding loans and "in-kind" contributions—goods and services that are contributed instead of money.

Don't do double work. Design one system that meets both your internal organization needs and any reporting requirements. The finance coordinator, the campaign treasurer, and the attorney advising the campaign must agree on what information should be kept. Cooperation and respect for each other's needs are the keys to success.

In-Kind Contributions

Remember, every dollar you don't have to spend is as good as another dollar raised. Consider the possibilities of in-kind contributions every time you need equipment, supplies, or professional services. Keep this in mind when looking for office space and furniture to set up your headquarters. Investigate real estate brokers, law offices, local unions, or businesses who might contribute use of their phones after regular business hours or on weekends for phone banks. If you need photography, typesetting, or printing, try to find a supporter who will contribute these skills. Lawyers and accountants can also be asked to contribute services your campaign needs.

Whenever you plan an activity, look at each projected expense item and ask, "Is there someone who can donate this?" The smaller the cost, the easier it will be to find a donor. Small expenditures can quickly add up. If costs are avoided by getting in-kind contributions, you'll see a big difference in your budget.

Make sure you know the applicable state laws governing these in-kind contributions. These donations generally have to be reported just as cash contributions. Valuing in-kind gifts accurately is important. Also, be careful to comply with any state or local laws that may restrict campaign contributions from a corporation.

Conclusion

The competing demands for both candidate and volunteer time in a campaign are extensive. You will have to carefully balance these resources between programs to contact voters and activities to raise the necessary funds. If you have a carefully thought-out campaign plan you can do both well. That's what running to win is all about.

9

VOLUNTEERS

If you've read this far you have a good idea of the amount of work involved in running any campaign. Now we get to the question, "Who does the work?" The answer almost always is volunteers. Even those campaigns that have enough money to hire a staff for management positions rely heavily on volunteers to do the bulk of the work.

Your ability to recruit, motivate, and effectively use volunteers will determine how well you will be able to carry out your voter communication plans. Because personal contact is so effective, motivated volunteers can provide the margin of victory in campaigns that are significantly outspent.

Unfortunately, there are no shortcuts. You can't buy a campaign organization; you have to build one. The keys to success are:

- A compelling campaign message that encourages people to get involved

- Constant efforts to recruit workers integrated into *all* campaign activities

- Good management that ensures volunteers are used effectively

Campaigning is hard work. Very few people will do it just because it's an interesting way to spend a few hours each week.

Most do it because of commitment. They trust the candidate; they believe in what he or she stands for; and they are confident the candidate's election will make a difference. To inspire participation, the candidate must have a compelling theme and clear stands on issues that concern potential volunteers. The candidate's personality, style, and community ties must reinforce and encourage that participation.

Make the issue of citizen involvement work for you. Reinforce the message that the candidate will be responsive to citizen interests once elected by highlighting the important role volunteers play in your campaign.

A strong theme can motivate volunteers, just as it persuades voters, but because you're asking much more of volunteers, you have to provide more to sustain their involvement throughout the campaign. This requires good planning, organization, and management of the entire volunteer program. Too often volunteers quit before Election Day because a disorganized campaign wastes their time. Workers know when their efforts are both productive and appreciated. Good organization goes a long way toward increasing their commitment to the candidate and the campaign's chances of success.

The Volunteer Coordinator

The first step in setting up your volunteer program is to appoint someone to coordinate volunteer recruitment and management. Continuity in this position is vital. The job cannot be handled well if done by a different person each day.

The volunteer coordinator in a campaign is like the ringmaster in a three-ring circus. You need someone who is highly organized, has a near mania about details and follow-up, and can motivate others. The job requires someone personable enough to get along well with people yet strong enough to supervise them. It's a tall order, but the right person will become a key member of your management team.

Depending on the geography and size of your district, you may want to appoint assistant volunteer coordinators for each area in which there will be significant activity. Make an effort to find people who can commit a good deal of time to the campaign.

An alternate method is to rely on the local field coordinators to enlist their friends and neighbors for canvassing drives, phone banks, or events in their area. Recruiting for mailings and other activities in the campaign headquarters can be done from the central office.

The volunteer coordinator recruits and manages volunteers, but decisions about how volunteer resources are allocated should always be made by the campaign manager based on the campaign plan's outline of priorities and the timetable for all activities. These guidelines must be followed by the volunteer coordinator.

The Plan for Volunteer Activities

A well-organized campaign will first decide what needs to be done, and how many people will be required to do it, before it sets about recruiting volunteers—that is the function of the volunteer budget discussed in Chapter 3.

The volunteer budget estimates the number of people needed for each scheduled activity. To determine your basic recruiting goals simply add up the volunteer needs for all programs scheduled in each week. Include canvassing, phone banks, mailings, driving the candidate, office maintenance, and all special projects or fundraising events. Then break this figure down for each day and each unit of time (morning, afternoon, evening) when volunteers will be required.

Your goal is to meet the requirements for each activity while building your volunteer base to the total number that will be needed on Election Day for your GOTV program. To play it safe, set your recruiting goal 10 to 15 percent higher to allow for no-shows.

Of course, no campaign can be so precisely designed that recruitment will exactly match the projections in the volunteer budget. But the budget does set goals for each activity and time period of the campaign. Adjustments in programs can then be made depending on the success of your recruitment. Programs can be expanded or new activities added if you recruit more volunteers. Similarly, if you recruit fewer volunteers than projected, you can decide which programs to cut back.

As you plan for volunteers, consider how you will use both headquarters' and at-home volunteers. The headquarters' volunteer is a person who will do outdoor work, such as canvassing, or work at the campaign office or at another centralized location such as a phone bank. Most campaigns place a high premium on head-quarters' volunteers since they can be closely supervised.

However, you can also use motivated volunteers who work only from their homes. Although it takes more effort to supervise volunteers working at home, some of your best workers will be senior citizens, parents with young children, and others who fit into this category.

In planning volunteer activities, decide which jobs must be done at a central location and which ones can be done elsewhere. If the campaign headquarters is a small room in the campaign manager's home, space may be so limited that certain tasks must be farmed out. If you do not have the use of a centralized phone bank you may have to assign all phone canvassing to be done from individual homes.

Organizing to Handle Volunteers

To use volunteers efficiently advance preparation is mandatory. Follow three basic steps to help your activities run more smoothly:

- Prepare the necessary materials for volunteers to do specific tasks

- Develop a system for keeping track of volunteers and their assignments

- Set up the headquarters to provide good working conditions

Preparation of Volunteer Materials

Make kits with all the materials volunteers will need to carry out each activity in your campaign plan. These may include:
- Written instructions: It's helpful for a volunteer to be able to refer back to a sheet as a reminder, even if instructions are also given orally. List each step involved in the task, giving examples where necessary. Be sure to indicate the deadline or timeline for the assignment. For activities such as telephone or door-to-door canvassing, the instructions should also include a sample script.

The materials prepared for use by at-home volunteers should also include the name and telephone number of the person to call if there are any questions.

• The tools necessary to carry out a specific assignment: These could include postcards, voter registration lists, precinct maps, pencils or pens, etc.

• A simple report form to keep track of results: These forms must meet the information needs of the field director, finance coordinator, or other staff responsible for the project. These will vary for each activity, but all should provide adequate space to record specific data such as number of calls completed or households contacted.

Recordkeeping

Three forms that will help the coordinator organize the volunteer program are:

• Pledge cards

• Daily volunteer schedule sheets

• Volunteer request forms

Pledge Cards

Pledge cards serve two functions in the campaign: they provide a way for supporters to sign up to help, and they can also be used as a file record to keep track of volunteers. You need a simple system that enables you to quickly locate the right volunteer for each task.

In addition to name, address, and phone number, the pledge card should allow volunteers to indicate which days and hours they are available and any special skills they may have, such as typing or a second language if it will be important in your campaign. Leave a space to indicate whether the volunteer will work at headquarters or at home. It is also helpful to know whether volunteers can use their own cars for campaign activities.

Some campaigns combine the pledge card and the fundraising reply envelope (see Chapter 8). This method saves on printing bills, but it's often difficult to put sufficient information about volunteers on the flap of a multi-purpose envelope. If you use a separate fundraising envelope, and a supporter indicates that they will

SAMPLE PLEDGE CARD

YES, I will help elect Vincent Kane to the School Board!

Name _____ Ward _____ Precinct _____

Address _____ Bus. Phone _____

_____ Zip _____ Home Phone _____

Enclosed is my contribution of $ _____

I can volunteer: Mon   Tues   Wed   Thurs   Fri   Sat   Sun
    Mornings
    Afternoons
    Evenings

I can type ☐   I can work: at headquarters ☐
I have a car ☐   only at home   ☐

volunteer, either transfer the information to a pledge card or cut off the envelope flap and staple it to the pledge card, leaving the space at the bottom to indicate available times and skills.

Make duplicates of the completed cards. One set should be filed by precinct or geographic area to make it easy to identify volunteers for localized voter contact programs such as canvassing and telephoning. File the other set alphabetically.

Here's another case where a personal computer could greatly ease your recordkeeping. Data base programs, like dBase II, Datastar, and scores of others can store and code volunteers' names and print them out in whatever form you need.

Volunteer Daily Schedule Sheets

The volunteer coordinator also needs a form for keeping track of assignments. Refer to your volunteer budget to determine how many workers are needed for each activity and when. Transfer this information to a Daily Volunteer Schedule Sheet like the one on page 194. Leave spaces for the names of volunteers who will be assigned to each activity in each time period.

Volunteer Request Forms

There will always be some volunteer needs that can not be anticipated in advance. Certain activities may be added or expanded if more money is raised. Others may be modified when changes are made in the campaign plan. Develop a simple form similar to the

DAILY VOLUNTEER SCHEDULE SHEET — DATE:				
	Mornings	Afternoon	Evening	At Home
Candidate Driver				
Headquarters: Answer Phone				
Mailing				
Prepare Canvass Lists				
Door-to-Door Canvass				
Telephone Canvass				
Special Projects/Events				

one on page 195 so that the campaign manager or project coordinators can request additional volunteers when necessary.

Setting Up the Headquarters

Every campaign needs a headquarters. The space may vary from a storefront on a well-trafficked street to the manager's basement recreation room, but you must have a central location that serves as the nerve center for the campaign. Having one place where lists and records are kept and where volunteers can report to get assignments is essential to both organizational effectiveness and communication.

It is well worth the time and effort to arrange the headquarters, however small, to provide the best possible working conditions. Getting volunteers is one thing, keeping them is another. If the headquarters is an efficient and pleasant place to work, volunteers will be more motivated to come back.

VOLUNTEER REQUEST FORM

Type of Activity: _____

Number of Volunteers Needed: _____

Special Skills Required: _____

Transportation Required: _____

Date(s): _____

Time — From: _____ To: _____

PLEASE TURN IN REQUESTS   Requested by: _____
AT LEAST 5 DAYS IN
ADVANCE   Date submitted: _____

Determine how many telephones you will need and order them as far ahead as possible—installation can take many weeks. Most phone companies require a large deposit from political campaigns. If your headquarters is in a private home, you should install a separate line (or lines) from the residential phone.

Many people's first impression of the campaign will be the volunteer who answers the phone. This person should be friendly and knowledgeable and have a professional manner. Decide on a standard greeting such as, "Kane for City Council. May I help you?" and affix this script to each phone.

It's important to keep the headquarters clean. This can be difficult, especially in the hectic pace of the final weeks. Since most volunteers will be working at this time, all available space will have to be used efficiently. The closer you get to the election the more likely it is that interested voters will stop by to pick up literature and reporters will come in to do interviews. The headquarters should convey the image of a well-organized campaign.

Post campaign schedules and copies of press clippings at headquarters to keep all volunteers informed. This helps even part-time volunteers feel they are a vital part of the entire campaign.

Recruiting Volunteers

Once you have determined how many volunteers are needed to carry out the campaign plan and have organized systems to use them efficiently, the next task is recruitment.

The first rule of getting people to volunteer is to ask. Few people will step forward spontaneously. How many times have you heard the post-election comment, "I would have helped, but no one ever asked me"?

Effective recruiting requires careful planning in each of the six basic stages:

- Recruiting volunteers for leadership roles

- Recruiting friends and associates

- Developing a recruiting message

- Ongoing recruitment

- Including recruitment in all campaign programs

- Thank-you letters and confirming phone calls that solidify volunteer commitments to help.

Consider what resources are available to your campaign as you go through each step.

Recruiting Volunteers for Leadership Roles

Recruitment should begin as soon as the candidate decides to run. It is very important to contact key people early, before they commit themselves to another campaign. You will need to find volunteers to fill important campaign leadership positions. At this early stage you are looking for individuals with particular skills and experience and a strong commitment and loyalty to the candidate. This core group of "middle managers" forms the base of the volunteer program and will be important in subsequent recruiting efforts. Some, such as Finance Committee members, are the foundation for your fundraising efforts. Others, such as ward or town coordinators, will be the volunteer leadership in your field organization. If you're not familiar with their qualifications check volunteers' reliability by monitoring performance on early activities before making permanent leadership assignments.

Recruiting Friends and Associates

Initial recruitment always begins with friends, relatives, and close associates of the candidate. As one campaign veteran put it, "If you don't have enough friends to launch a respectable campaign, you probably couldn't win anyway. Your friends know you best." The candidate should go through personal phone lists, Christmas card lists, directories of former classmates, and business and political associates to identify people who can be asked to help in the campaign.

Next, go over the membership lists of all the civic associations, clubs, and organizations you belong to or have worked with. When you add up all the groups, the numbers may surprise you. One candidate for Board of Supervisors in San Francisco discovered that she was affiliated with more than forty organizations and was an active member in more than half of them. These included such groups as the League of Women Voters, the Women's Political Caucus, the PTA, the NAACP, a neighborhood association, Business and Professional Women, and her church group. She made a list of the ten most likely volunteers in each organization and personally called each one of them. In less than a week's time, she recruited 120 volunteers!

Later in the campaign you can contact organizations that have endorsed or indicated support for your candidate and work out a system to involve their members as campaign volunteers. In some cases unions or community organizations may recruit their own members to perform specific campaign activities. In other instances they will provide you with a membership list that you will have to solicit.

Recruiting Message

When reaching beyond friends and associates who have a personal relationship with the candidate, a standard "pitch" is helpful for recruiting volunteers. This message must be short and persuasive. Your pitch must suit your own personal style, but these are the basic ingredients:

• Information about the candidate and why he or she should be elected: Your recruiting pitch is essentially a variation of your basic campaign theme.

• Information about the activities that volunteers will be doing: This is often needed to show newcomers they don't need special skills or experience to work in a campaign. Stress how important volunteers are to your election effort.

• Specific time requests: Ask which days and times are best.

Try to get a commitment for as much time as you can. It is important to leave the impression that the campaign is well-organized and that a volunteer's time will be put to good use.

In some cases the pitch should be specialized to emphasize the candidate's position on issues that are of interest to a prospective volunteer. For example, when contacting retired citizens, stress the candidate's record or proposals for senior citizens' programs. Even though their issues may not be a central campaign theme, develop special appeals to recruit members of active constituencies or issue groups such as environmentalists, nurses, neighborhood groups, women's organizations, businesspeople, and the like.

Ongoing Recruitment

The candidate plays a crucial recruiting role in the early stages, but once an initial base is built, don't stop recruiting. Everyone, including the candidate, should feel responsible for bringing new people into the campaign. Indeed, volunteers who think the campaign is worth their time shouldn't be bashful about asking others to get involved. Make sure every campaign worker has a supply of pledge cards. You can use the pyramid pledge system described in the fundraising chapter—each new volunteer pledges to recruit so many others—to keep the numbers growing.

The second level of recruiting also involves systematic telephone contact with potential volunteers. Develop a plan to call members of civic, political, and issue-oriented organizations in your district with your recruiting message. This network will yield many activists who should be encouraged to play a role in the campaign. If you have campaign supporters who belong to particular groups, get them to make calls to other members. The more personal the contact, the greater the chance of success.

If ballot access petitions are used in your district, don't overlook the people who signed your petition. Each can be called or sent a pledge card with a letter from the candidate asking them to get involved with the campaign.

Workers from past campaigns in your area are a great resource. Competition for experienced volunteers will be especially high when there are many races on the ballot. Try to get volunteer lists from former candidates who are not running this year. These candidates, or their campaign managers, can identify particularly well-qualified workers.

Sometimes it is effective to place recruitment notices on bulletin boards at colleges or high schools. Better yet, appoint an assistant volunteer recruiter at each high school or college to sign up additional students. First-time, school-age volunteers can often be trained to perform important campaign jobs such as canvassing. And they're enthusiastic workers for the unlimited number of unskilled jobs that only require willing hands. You may want to contact professors to see if it is possible to arrange credit for students who work in your campaign.

Including Volunteer Recruitment in All Campaign Programs

Your recruiting efforts will be greatly expanded if you include an appeal for workers in every aspect of the campaign's activities. Literature, direct mail, candidate speeches, canvassing scripts, and all other contacts with voters should incorporate efforts to recruit volunteers.

One way to do this is to include a volunteer pledge card in all campaign mailings. The address of campaign headquarters can be printed on the reverse side so the supporter who is willing to give volunteer time can simply mail it back. All other printed campaign material, including leaflets and newspaper ads, can contain a statement, such as: "Your help is needed to elect (candidate) to the School Board. Please call (phone #) or come to the campaign headquarters at (address) to volunteer."

Appearances by the candidate are one of the most effective ways to recruit volunteers. A voter's interest in the campaign is usually at its height immediately after meeting the candidate. A campaign organization should be prepared to take full advantage of this situation. At any speech, meeting or event make clear that the campaign needs members of the audience to become involved. The candidate should carry pledge cards and a staff aide should note the name and telephone number of anyone who expresses even tentative interest. These people should be contacted the following day to confirm their commitment and find out the times and days they will be available to work.

Whether canvassing is conducted door-to-door or over the telephone, no contact with a friendly voter is complete without asking, "Can you give us a few hours per week to assist the campaign?'' Strike while the iron is hot. As soon as the voter expresses an interest in the campaign, seek a volunteer commitment.

No campaign ever has too many volunteers. If your campaign is well-planned and organized, you can make effective use of as many volunteers as you can get. The recruitment process should continue right up to Election Day.

Follow-Up

As soon as each volunteer is recruited, a thank-you letter from the candidate should be sent. This will firm up the volunteer's commitment and demonstrate that the help is greatly valued. Don't overlook this simple way to motivate campaign volunteers. You can use a simple form letter, but each should be signed by the candidate:

SAMPLE VOLUNTEER THANK-YOU LETTER

Dear (name of volunteer),

I deeply appreciate your willingness to help me in this campaign. Volunteers like yourself will really make the difference.

We have a lot of work ahead but together we can win on November 3.

Sincerely,

(Candidate)

Each volunteer who signs a pledge card or indicates a willingness to help should receive a phone call from the volunteer coordinator within a few days. The call should seek a specific commitment of days and times when the volunteer will work. Stress how serious volunteer assignments are and how much the campaign relies on the individual's involvement. These time commitments provide the information you'll need to plan work schedules and make assignments. If you receive a firm commitment for even a few hours, schedule the volunteer for an activity as soon as it is possible.

There's always work to do to prepare for the major activities that will take place when the campaign is in full swing. Tasks include looking up phone numbers for the telephone canvass or preparing walking lists for the door-to-door canvass. Some campaigns have volunteers write personal endorsement cards to friends within the district. Have these projects ready for volunteers who sign up early. If they become actively involved, volunteers are likely to increase their time commitment to the campaign.

The follow-up call also serves another purpose: weeding out people who have changed their minds or who really do not have the time or inclination to help in the campaign. It is better to get such people off the list early than to count on them at a crucial time.

Managing the Volunteer Program

Now that you have recruited volunteers, you need to develop a management system to use them in campaign activities. The three parts of the system are: making volunteer assignments, providing training, and monitoring the results.

Making Assignments

To begin making assignments, go through the pledge cards and match available volunteers with each activity in the volunteer daily schedule. It's best to assign a few extra workers to important projects to cover for no-shows. This is especially true in the early stages of the campaign, before you've had a chance to check volunteers' reliability. Record a volunteer's name and phone number next to each assigned task. This will provide a handy list for the volunteer coordinator or an assistant to call to confirm the assignments. It also helps to send a postcard or simple form letter like the one on page 202 to let volunteers know when they are scheduled to work.

Post copies of the schedules for the entire week in a prominent place in the headquarters so volunteers can check it regularly. Give a copy to the field director or other coordinators supervising projects.

SAMPLE VOLUNTEER CARD

Thank you for volunteering to help elect (candidate). I'll be counting on you for the following activities:

Date	Activity	Time From: To:	Report to

Please call (name) at (phone #) if you will be unable to come or if you have any questions.

Sincerely,

Volunteer Coordinator

If you have planned an extensive GOTV program you will need the largest number of volunteers on Election Day. Anyone who can possibly take off from work should be asked well in advance to reserve at least a part of that day for campaign activities.

How clearly volunteers understand their assigned tasks can make or break your whole program. Volunteers who are given confusing, disorganized instructions will not wait around for a second assignment. Each volunteer assignment should include clear, step-by-step instructions. Be specific. Let the campaign worker know exactly what is expected: the number of calls to be made, the number of postcards to be written, the way to record results, and so on. The instructions should also state a deadline for completing the job.

Never give volunteers more than they can handle. If they can't see their way through to the end of the task, they are likely to loose interest. Being asked to canvass the whole west side of town can be overwhelming. A list of fifty houses, on the other hand, is manageable. Ask volunteers to write twenty-five letters, not 250. The percentage of jobs completed will be much greater. Volunteers are more likely to take on another assignment when they have successfully completed one.

Volunteers who understand the importance of each task will feel more motivated to do the countless hours of necessary detail work. Help them recognize how instrumental their efforts are in carrying out the campaign plan. Tell volunteers the purpose of the mailing they are addressing or explain the targeting process that selected the precincts they are canvassing.

Volunteer Training

For individual jobs, the written instructions included in the volunteer kit are probably sufficient. But for a major project, such as phone banks or canvassing, it is advisable to hold a training session for those volunteers who will be involved. This becomes absolutely necessary for voter contact activities where you want to make sure every volunteer delivers the same message in the same way.

Start each training session by explaining the purpose of the activity and what role it plays in the overall campaign. Volunteers will feel more involved if they understand how their task fits into the whole. Stimulate enthusiasm by setting reasonable goals—numbers of calls, pieces of literature distributed, and so on—for each group to reach. Your aim here is not to build competition, but to give each worker a goal to attain.

Instructions for the activity should be very specific. All materials used by volunteers should be reviewed by the trainer. Give the volunteers additional confidence by going through the task step-by-step, role playing a telephone call to an undecided voter, or talking with a voter in a door-to-door canvass. Answer any questions and discuss how to handle any problems that may arise.

For first-time campaign volunteers this type of group training is especially helpful. It is reassuring to know that they are not the only ones who will be knocking on doors. But even with experienced campaign veterans, training assures that the activity will be done in a manner consistent with your campaign plan.

Monitoring the Results

The coordinator responsible for each activity needs numerical results so the campaign's progress can be measured. Periodic feedback is vital to evaluate the effectiveness of each program and to make any necessary adjustments. For this reason, the field director and the finance coordinator must receive accurate records of the work accomplished by volunteers. The report forms that are included in the volunteer kits should request specific information and be turned in regularly. (See the sample canvassing report form on page 93.)

The volunteer coordinator should also review the results reported on these forms to evaluate each volunteer's performance. Monitoring is particularly important when you have a large number of volunteers who are working at home without direct supervision. Set short intervals for volunteers to report on their progress. If a job isn't being done, you want to know as soon as possible so that the task can be reassigned.

Sustaining a Volunteer Organization

A great deal of effort and patience is needed to sustain a volunteer organization throughout a campaign. Volunteers give their time primarily because they want to help your candidate. But many also have personal needs that figure into the equation. Meeting some of those needs will go a long way toward motivating volunteers and keeping them actively involved in the campaign.

Most important is the need for recognition. Volunteers should feel that their efforts are noticed and appreciated, and that the campaign couldn't make it without each one of them. Thank-you letters sent to volunteers when they are recruited is a good first step. As the campaign progresses and individuals complete big projects, send other thank-you letters.

Brief handwritten notes from the candidate are especially effective. Another good morale booster is acknowledging a volunteer who is in charge of an important project with an appropriate title.

Campaign volunteers can also be recognized in a way that gets press coverage for the campaign. The press secretary should issue news releases announcing the appointment of volunteers to campaign leadership roles, such as precinct coordinators and organizers of major fundraising events. Especially in a district with small local papers, these releases are frequently printed. The stories add a personal dimension to the campaign.

Periodic meetings where the candidate updates volunteers on the campaign's progress are good ways to make everyone feel an integral part of the effort. The candidate can also help motivate workers by spending time in headquarters speaking informally with volunteers and occasionally participating in a big project, such as putting out a mass mailing. The atmosphere created by the candidate, campaign manager, and volunteer coordinator should emphasize the importance to the campaign of volunteer work.

Make the volunteer's job as enjoyable as possible. Try to plan work to be done in groups at the headquarters or another central location whenever possible. Camaraderie makes a task seem easier and go more quickly than working alone at home.

Parties are another good way to boost morale. At the end of a long project plan a small get-together as a reward. It's important that the candidate attend some of these. For most campaigns the election night victory party is the final celebration. Indeed, success is the best reward for everyone, but candidates who are serious about sustaining a volunteer organization will find further ways to thank volunteers and keep them involved. Consider sending a personal note or letter to all volunteers, or hosting a "thank you party" after the candidate takes office. Remember, these people will not only be active supporters once you're in office, they are the first people you'll contact when you start your reelection campaign.

BIBLIOGRAPHY
AND RESOURCES

Campaigns & Elections, Box 807, 1621 Brookside Road, McLean, Va. 22101, (703) 534-7774. A quarterly journal with excellent nuts and bolts articles on all aspects of campaigns. Subscription: 1 yr., $48.

The following is a selection of *C&E* reprints especially applicable to state and local races:

A1008. "Impact Polling: Feedback for a Winning Strategy," by Tubby Harrison. Why current political polling is inadequate; examines turnout, impact of issues, and degree of voter commitment. $1.50 each.

A2049. "How to Get Elected to Your State Legislature," by Hank Parkinson. Valuable advice to any challenger or incumbent. $2.50 each.

A7024. "Printing: How to Get the Most for Your Campaign Literature Dollar," by Lorene Hanley Duquin. $3.50 each.

A9015. "Door-to-Door Campaigning: How to Get the Most Out of Your Pedometer," by Lorene Hanley Duquin. The benefits and bothers of door-to-door candidate visits are spelled out. $3.50 each.

A9025. "The Cost-Effectiveness of Grass-Roots Campaign Activities," by John Berrigan, Ph.D. $3.50 each.

A9037. "Rural Campaigning: The Neglected 'New Frontier,'" by Kelly Ross. The author discusses how to campaign in a rural area. $3.50 each.

A13011. "Electoral Targeting, Part I: For the Do-It-Yourself Campaign," by Murray Fishel. How to get and begin quantifying critical data; basic worksheets are included. $5.00 each.

A14004. "Electoral Targeting II: Analyzing the Data," by Murray Fishel. A teaching manaul on analyzing electoral data for targeting campaign resources. $5.00 each.

A14020. "Working a Room: The Basic Rules," by Lorene Hanley Duquin. Advice on meeting voters—for the novice as well as the old hand. $2.50 each.

A17020. "New Absentee and Mail-In Ballot Campaigns: The Winning Edge," by Martha Walrath-Riley. Learn how to increase turnout, guarantee votes, and swing elections. $5.00 each.

A19018. "The Pluses and Minuses of Do-it-Yourself Polling," by Lorene Hanley Duquin. What you need to know to get an in-house polling operation up and running. $4.50 each.

The following *C&E* reprints offer simplified instructions for using computers in campaigns:

A11069. "Microcomputers: Their Use in Small-Scale Political Campaigning," by Joyhn R. Tkach, M.S., M.D. How an Apple II was used for targeting in a school board referendum campaign. $2.50 each.

A12129. "Portable Computers: Useful in Statewide Campaigns," by Dan Frahm and Jon Mosle. $3.50 each.

A14066. "Micro Software for Campaign List Management Programs," by Rita Risser. Computer list-building tips. $2.50 each.

A15073. "Targeting with Visiclc: Using an Electronic Spreadsheet in a Local Campaign," by Frank Rogers. $3.50 each.

A16075. "Running for Mayor with a Micro: How Computer Volunteer Training Paid off in Charlotte," by Allyn McGillicuddy and Vernon L. Robinson. $4.50 each.

A16082. "Ballots & Bytes: Getting Started with Micros," by John Tkach. $3.50 each.

A18056. "New Techniques in Computerized Voter Contact," by Frank Tobe. The science of political database development from one of the leading innovators. $4.50 each.

Democratic National Committee, 20 Ivy Street, S.E., Washington, D.C. 20003, (202) 863–8000. The DNC produces excellent campaign manuals, though most are designed primarily for candidates and the staffs of large—congressional and statewide—campaigns. Contact the DNC and your state Democratic party office for more information on current materials and training sessions that are available.

Republican National Committee, 310 First Street, S.E., Washington, D.C. 20003, (202) 863–8500. The Political Education Department offers seminars for campaign managers and press secretaries on a regional basis. The RNC also publishes updated versions of their campaign manuals for Republican candidates every two years.

National Committee for an Effective Congress, 505 C Street, N.E., Washington, D.C. 20002, (202) 547–1151. NCEC's *Guide to Effective Campaigns* is written primarily for congressional campaigns, but contains good material that is useful at any level.

Campaign Treasurer's Handbook, published by the American Institute of Certified Public Accountants, 1211 Avenue of the Americas, New York, N.Y. 10036. A helpful guide to campaign financial recordkeeping.

Agranoff, Robert. *The Management of Election Campaigns.* Boston: Holbrook Press, 1976. According to the author, "The book is devoted to the principle that political science does have something to contribute to those interested in practical politics." It definitely does. A good general reference book.

Chester, Marjorie F. *McCall's Book of Fundraising Ideas.* Englewood Cliffs, N.J.: Prentice-Hall, 1963. The majority of ideas in this compendium are timeless. Well worth hunting down.

Gaby, Daniel M., and Merle H. Treusch. *Election Campaign Handbook.* Englewood Cliffs, N.J.: Prentice-Hall, 1976. This detailed collection of campaign techniques provides sample graphics for campaign literature and ready-to-use forms.

Kent, Frank. *The Great Game of Politics.* New York: Doubleday, 1923. This book is good historic reading. It's intriguing to see how much—and how little—electoral strategies have advanced in more than half a century.

Parkinson, Hank. *Winning Your Campaign: A Nuts-and-Bolts Guide to Political Victory.* Englewood Cliffs, N.J.: Prentice-Hall, 1970. This book provides one of the best guides to the public realtions aspects of campaigning, particularly announcing candidacy, press releases and conferences, and campaign scheduling. Parkinson provides invaluable information and insights to the potential candidate.

Roll, Charles, and Albert Cantrill.*Polls: Their Use and Misuse in Politics.* New York: Basic Books, 1972. A good basic primer to evaluate the utility of polling data in local campaigns.

Roper, William L. *Winning Politics: A Handbook for Candidates and Campaign Workers.* Radnor, Penn.: Chilton Book Company, 1978.

Schwartz, Cipora O. *How to Run A School Board Campaign and Win.* Wilde Lake Village Green, Columbia, Md.: The National Committee for Citizens in Education, 1982.

Simpson, Dick. *Winning Elections: A Handbook in Participatory Politics.* Chicago: Swallow Press, 1972. Practical suggestions for local campaigns based on the experience of the Independent Precinct Organization in Chicago by former Alderman Simpson.

The following organizations are good leads for additional materials, and in some cases sources of funds, for women candidates:

National Women's Education Fund, 1410 Que Street, N.W., Washington, D.C. 20009, (202) 462–8606. NWEF offers a series of campaign training sessions for women candidates at the state and local level as well as skills workshops for women elected officials. They also publish an excellent comprehensive *Campaign Handbook* (1978) written especially for women candidates. Cost is $18.00. Further information on services is available from their Washington office.

Women's Campaign Fund, 815 15th Street, N.W., Suite 601, Washington, D.C. 20005, (202) 638–3900. WCF provides technical support and direct PAC contributions to women candidates. Most of their resources are concentrated at the congressional and statewide level, but they can provide assistance to key local women candidates.

National Women's Political Caucus, 1275 K Street, N.W., Suite 750, Washington, D.C. 20002, (202) 898-1100. At their national convention in June 1985, NWPC offered a day-long Advanced Political Training Seminar for women candidates and their campaign managers. They also publish a *How to Press and PR Handbook*. Contact the national office for further information on available materials and for the contact person for your state chapter.

National Organization for Women, 1401 New York Avenue, N.W., Washington, D.C. 20005, (202) 347-2279. Local NOW chapters endorse candidates and some provide training sessions for state and local races. Contact the national office for further information.

League of Women Voters, 1730 M Street, N.W., Washington, D.C. 20036, (202) 429-1965. Each state and local LWV chapter operates independently. Contact the national office for the name of the president in your area. The League also publishes a short *Campaign Handbook*, available from their Washington office.

National Federation of Republican Women, 310 First Street, S.E., Washington, D.C. 20003, (202) 863-8200. NFRW offers a two-and-a-half day Campaign Management School on effective campaign techniques and the unique aspects of women running for elective office. Open to all interested Republicans, men and women. Course registration fee is approximately $100. They also publish two booklets for the first-time woman candidate: *Consider Yourself for Public Office* ($2.50 each) and *Campaign Manual* ($2.00 each).

Paizis, Suzanne. *Getting Her Elected*. Sacramento, Calif.: Creative Editions, 1977.

Ms Magazine, "Look Before You Leap," April 1974, p. 67. Contains a bibliography of resources for potential women candidates.

INDEX